The Idea of a Christian School

The Idea of a Christian School

And Why It Matters for the Child You Love

TOM STONER

Foreword by Philip Graham Ryken

CASCADE *Books* · Eugene, Oregon

THE IDEA OF A CHRISTIAN SCHOOL
And Why It Matters for the Child You Love

Cascade Books
An Imprint of Wipf and Stock Publishers
199 W. 8th Ave., Suite 3
Eugene, OR 97401

www.wipfandstock.com

PAPERBACK ISBN: 979-8-3852-1294-1
HARDCOVER ISBN: 979-8-3852-1295-8
EBOOK ISBN: 979-8-3852-1296-5

Cataloguing-in-Publication data:

Names: Stoner, Tom, author. | Philip Graham Ryken, foreword.

Title: The idea of a Christian school : and why it matters for the child you love / Tom Stoner; foreword by Philip Graham Ryken.

Description: Eugene, OR: Cascade Books, 2024 | Includes bibliographical references and index.

Identifiers: ISBN 979-8-3852-1294-1 (paperback) | ISBN 979-8-3852-1295-8 (hardcover) | ISBN 979-8-3852-1296-5 (ebook)

Subjects: LCSH: Christian education. | Education (Christian theology). | Education—Philosophy.

Classification: BV1471.2 S85 2024 (paperback) | BV1471.2 (ebook)

05/10/24

To the memory of Richard F. Gross,
sixth president of Gordon College, Wenham, Massachusetts.

Known as "Biggie" to family and friends, Dick was a man of tall stature in every sense of the word. After experiencing the power of Christian schooling as a student at Wheaton College, he gave his career to the work of translating the idea of a Christian school into reality for the sake of the students in his care, including nearly three decades at Gordon. "Holy shoddy is still shoddy" was more than a phrase he coined and was known to repeat, it reflects a priority of his leadership and captures a measure of his life and legacy.

After retiring from Gordon, Dick and his wife, Jody, gave all of their best to Covenant Christian Academy, where their grandchildren were among the many outstanding students. Dick chaired the board and served as a catalyst for expansion, growth, and change. During these years, Dick and I spent countless hours together, and he and Jody became treasured friends to my whole family. He was to me the definition of a mentor and he left an indelible mark upon my life for which I will be forever grateful.

Contents

CONTENTS

List of Illustrations

Foreword

A student from a Christian elementary school in West Philadelphia threw his backpack down at the end of a long school day and complained, "It's all the same!"

Sensing a challenge, the child's mother wanted to learn more: "What do you mean, 'It's all the same'?" she asked.

"Church, home, school—it's all the same!" the boy said. After further questioning, it emerged that the young scholar was tired of learning the same moral, spiritual, and intellectual lessons everywhere he went—in all three of his primary communities.

"Yes, it's the same!" his mother declared. "That's the plan, so get used to it!"

Rather than opening the door to divided loyalties, the child's mother wisely upheld biblical values in every sphere of her son's social connections. She knew that when children are educated in a consistently Christian context—including school as well as home and church—they get a chance to see how "all things hold together" in Jesus Christ (Colossians 1:17). They also receive the best possible preparation to make a difference in the world for the kingdom of God.

The Idea of a Christian School articulates the vital role that strong Christian schools can play in spiritual formation. By reinforcing what Christian parents are modeling in the home and what pastors proclaim at church, Christ-centered schools help provide the total educational discipleship that every child needs. This is true spiritually and theologically, of course, but it is also true intellectually. Christian education is needed for the full discipleship of the Christian mind.

The wise tradition of Christian education is deeply rooted in the history of the church. Already in the early centuries of Christendom, believers in influential cities such as Antioch and Alexandria wanted their young people to get the best possible education—in those days, the liberal arts training pioneered and prized by the ancient Greeks.

By the early Middle Ages, the learned Alcuin had brought distinctively Christ-centered education to the courts of Charlemagne. In the following centuries, Christian schools spread across Europe, usually in close association with local churches.

Today, there are truly global networks of Christian schools, such as the Association of Christian Schools International. Most Americans are within reach of a good Christian elementary, middle, or high school. Millions of African children are educated in church-affiliated schools. Even in such spiritually closed countries as China, there is unprecedented interest in Christian schooling. Parents always want the best for their children, and for the Christian community, that means establishing thriving classrooms everywhere Jesus is honored as Lord.

Tom Stoner has drunk deeply from the life-giving wells of Christ-centered learning. At Wheaton College, we studied together under professors who had a rare passion for Christian education. Tom took Greek with Gerald Hawthorne and English with Joe McClatchey. He also read the philosophy of Arthur Holmes, whose book *The Idea of the Christian College* champions "an education that cultivates the creative and active integration of faith and learning."

Stoner has drawn abundantly from these living waters in his faithful leadership at influential Christian schools in Boston, St. Louis, and Chicago. In this book he shares his well-tested reflections on the importance of integrating the Christian faith with every aspect of Christian schooling, both inside and outside the classroom.

Whereas many previous books on faith and learning have focused on colleges and universities, *The Idea of a Christian School* brings the best traditions of Christian education to elementary and secondary schools.

Think of the book as a *primer*, or short introduction to a field of study, where important concepts are clearly explained and practically applied. What is the Christian worldview? How do we educate the whole person? How can teachers facilitate more integrative moments in the classroom, when their students can see how academic subjects intersect with the life of faith?

The Idea of a Christian School also asks deeper questions. What does it mean to "think Christianly"? What are the implications of bearing the divine image for how teachers teach, and students learn? How can Christian education achieve its ultimate purpose, which Frank Gaebelein defined as "integration into the all-embracing truth of God"?

This book is for educators who teach in Christian schools, helping them to understand the forms of intellectual training and spiritual formation that will empower their students for lifelong discipleship. It is also for administrators who cast a comprehensive educational vision for their schools, inspired by the life transformation that takes place when teachers and students connect.

This book is also to share with parents and grandparents who are considering Christian schools. Is Christ-centered education worth the costly investment it usually requires?

This question was answered again for me when a young woman from China walked into my office and told me her life story.

Her parents were church planters, who educated their precious daughter at underground Christian schools, knowing that as a result she would never be allowed to attend university in China. As an act of faith, they sent her to complete her education in the United States. Remarkably—almost miraculously—God provided everything she needed to attend a Christian high school and then matriculate at college.

Now she was at Wheaton, studying to be a teacher. Her goal? To go back to China and give other children the same priceless gift that she had received: a thoroughly Christ-centered education.

Such an education, she knew, would strengthen students at school with the same faith they were taught at home, witnessed in the church, and would be called to share with the world.

PHILIP RYKEN
President
Wheaton College

Acknowledgments

This book was made possible by a series of people and life events beginning in fall, 1955, when my father, Del Stoner, enrolled at the University of Minnesota. He took classes for a semester then worked full-time to earn money to take more classes, and repeated this cycle until he graduated in June, 1961, the first person in his family to go to college. Soon a job offer from the ServiceMaster corporation took my parents and their young family to Wheaton, Illinois. They continued to prioritize the value of schooling for their children, giving me the opportunities and experiences I write about here.

Several years after I finished seminary, Jane Wells gave me the name of Dr. Charles Glenn, the chair of the department of education at Boston University. She told me "Charlie" enjoyed taking Christian students under his wing and I found that truer words have rarely been spoken. He was instrumental in every aspect of my experience at BU and became a friend to my whole family. When I reached the dissertation stage, he pointed me in the direction of the research reflected in the pages of this book.

This was my first experience working with a professional editor but it is hard for me to imagine someone better than Evelyn Bence. I owe a debt of gratitude to her and to Bruce Lockerbie, a longtime consultant for Christian schools, for recommending her to me.

Bill Hughes and Robb Johnson, two entrepreneurs and friends in St. Louis, gave me office space in their respective companies during the year when I worked full-time writing this book.

Dan Treier may have been the biggest advocate of this project's publication. His personal encouragement and professional contacts helped make it a reality.

I owe a debt of gratitude to many colleagues and friends laboring in Christian schools, and especially the teachers, fellow administrators, board members, parents, and students at each of the schools where I have worked: Covenant Christian Academy in Peabody, MA; Westminster Christian Academy in Town and Country, MO; and Covenant Classical School in Naperville, IL, whose ideas and examples fill these pages.

My wife, Carrie, and our children—Lauren, Emily, David, and Jonny—have walked a long path with me and been constant sources of joy and encouragement along the way.

Finally, the great Christian mathematician and astronomer Johannes Kepler famously said the study of science is an effort to "think God's thoughts after him." By extension, the same can be said not just of students' efforts in school, but all of humanity's attempts throughout time to understand the truth of all created realities. How then might I properly acknowledge the one who hung the stars and continues to uphold the universe by the word of his power?

Words fail but I do wish to acknowledge this: in times of deep struggle throughout my research and writing, I often could manage only the simple prayer, "Help me, God." What profit readers find in the pages that follow might appropriately be viewed as an answer to that prayer. I am, of course, responsible for any limitations.

Tom Stoner
Naperville, Illinois
Spring 2024

Introduction

If you've ever asked the question, "I wonder what difference a Christian school might make in my child's or my grandchild's life?," this book is for you. I have spent more than twenty-five years as a head of three different Christian schools; sixteen near Boston, three in St. Louis, Missouri, and seven and counting near Chicago.

In these years, I have hired some hundred teachers and interviewed hundreds more. In nearly every interview, I ask, "What do you see as the advantage of teaching in a Christian school?" The most common response to this question is some variation of "I think it would be great to be able to be open with my students about my personal faith." The answer doesn't satisfy me.

One conversation with a sharp young Christian woman has stuck with me. She had recently graduated with an education major from one of our nation's top public universities and broke the news that she had just landed her first job as a classroom teacher in a public school! After a hearty "congratulations!" and spontaneous celebration, I asked curiously, "Did you ever consider teaching in a Christian school?" She replied, "A lot of the teachers in this public school are Christians so it is kind of like a Christian school." *She's missing the underlying foundation of Christian schooling*, I thought.

Although it is true that most teachers in Christian schools acknowledge having made personal commitments to Christian faith, and they certainly have the freedom to speak openly about their personal faith, these facts do not capture the idea of a Christian school. My dissatisfaction with such responses is compounded in professional circles when I too often hear and read poorly articulated philosophies of Christian-school education; I see colleagues around the world wrestling with the same questions while calling for clarity. But then I admit that my dissatisfaction with the articulation of others has been tempered at times by my own muddled thinking about the topic at hand: what really makes a Christian school distinctive—in philosophy and practice—from public schools and other private schools? To ask it another way, what are Christian schools trying to do, and what difference does it make for the students who attend them?

After thirteen years as the head of a Christian school in Boston, I initiated doctoral research focused on preparing teachers to promote distinctive Christian schools. I'll never forget sitting in the Boston University library day after day reading the literature on Christian-school philosophy, the concept of a worldview, and the integration of faith in learning. I valued aha! moments when I gained new insights. There I caught a glimpse into the breadth and depth of the idea of a Christian school. These are the thoughts I share with you here.

Given my experience of discovering how inadequate my own idea of Christian schooling proved to be, despite my personal and professional involvement, it is also possible that your preconceptions do not fully capture the idea and value of a Christian school. If this proves to be true, a child you know and love may benefit from your consideration of the ideas I present here.

Because of the book's goal, I deliberately chose the title to echo the monumental work of the nineteenth-century theologian and educator, John Henry Newman: *The Idea of a University*. Newman defined the soul of the Catholic university. My goal is to summarize and further define the soul of the Christian school. In sharp contrast to the massive scope of Newman's work, this book is a primer, a short introduction to the ideas that make Christian schools different. Volumes have been and will continue to be written on each idea I briefly address.

If asked, "Who is the target audience for this book?" I would quickly say parents and grandparents. I write these words for the people who count the care of children among their highest callings and privileges—providing for their needs, desiring their best, and seeking to impart to them every advantage for a life well lived. For you I wish to ask and answer the question, In what ways might a Christian school be a very helpful partner in your efforts and contribute to the cultivation of your child's mind and heart day in and day out? For those who have their children in Christian schools, may this bolster your appreciation of the experience and the value of your investment.

Though the center of my target audience is parents and grandparents, I foresee readers to include the thousands of *practitioners* in the Christian schooling arena—teachers, coaches, directors, administrators, board members, staff, and volunteers—who give all your best to produce and advance the mission of Christian schools in the lives of students worldwide. I trust that I can contribute information and inspiration that will deepen your personal commitment to this worthy endeavor and information to help you promote the distinctive nature of Christian schools. I would love one day for these ideas to be so widely understood in the field of Christian schooling that they begin to sound like "See Spot run" from the Basal readers of old.

Finally, I write for students preparing for a career in the field of education, facing a choice of the best-fit school from among the many available options for your career. May these ideas help inform your choice.

As we get started, I want to provide a spoiler alert: I believe deeply in the power and value of Christian schooling. After a good experience in the local public school through eighth grade, I followed my older sister and chose to attend a Christian high school. These years shaped my life. To this day I look forward to seeing classmates, teachers, and coaches at reunions. In our children my wife and I have also witnessed the impact of Christian schooling. And for more than two and a half decades, I have welcomed returning graduates from schools where I have served—graduates who are influencing the world for Christ and his truth; I hear them say, "My years here helped me become the person I am today." I hope that these pages help you see more clearly why this is true.

I

The Power of Education

Why Selecting a Child's School Is So Important

"To be human is to seek to find answers to questions about the world in which we live, and the answers we seek are the truth: they correspond to the way things really are."

—TOM STONER

"Real education always rests upon an understanding of what is required for human beings to flourish, to be all they are capable of being. And that involves making choices among competing visions."

—CHARLES L. GLENN

Education is one of the most powerful influences in our lives. Think for a moment about the people and experiences that have helped you become the person you are today. Did the name of a teacher, coach, director, or other staff person from your years in school come to mind? Or perhaps you are thinking of an experience you had at school or a school-related activity that helped you discover a passion or talent, a career or life purpose.

Not all of our school experiences are life shaping in a positive sense. Some unpleasant experiences we wish to forget. The point is that our experiences in school mark us beyond the facts we learned about math, science, and social studies. Our schooling shapes who we are because it influences what we believe about ourselves, about others, and about the world in which we live. Have you ever wondered why this is true?

THE GOAL OF EDUCATION: HELPING STUDENTS PUT THE PIECES TOGETHER

As we consider what makes our schooling so formative we might easily focus on the simple fact that children spend seven hours a day at school. Multiply this by an average of 170 or more school days, and we find that students spend 1,200+ hours a year at school! This fact alone is revealing; doing that much of anything is influential. But there is more to it than mere time.

From the moment of birth (actually, I imagine this begins even before birth), a child begins to construct an understanding of the world. There is no need to assign the child the task to do this; rather, it is part of what it means to be human. Our senses provide a near constant stream of data, and our minds analyze and interpret the data in an effort to make sense of it and determine its meaning. In many ways, this process of assembling pieces of data together to construct an understanding of the world is similar to as-sembling a gigantic (world-sized!) puzzle. The pieces are the wide-ranging bits of information children receive: ideas, emotions, experiences, facts, knowledge, etc., and the picture they are assembling is their understanding of the world.

Schooling is a huge part of this puzzle assembly. The process of edu-cation is designed to be a developmental activity in which children learn from their teachers, coaches, peers, textbooks, and other sources what they do not know about the world. This process of learning about the world at school, seven hours a day, 170 days a year, year after year, helps us begin to see why our children's schooling is so influential to their understanding of the world. But there is much more to it that will help us understand better the power of schooling.

WHAT KINDS OF QUESTIONS DOES A CHILD ASK?

To fully grasp the power of schooling it is crucial to understand the type of questions all children seek to answer. The human heart is preprogrammed to ask questions such as "What is the meaning of life? How'd we get here? What happens when we die? Why am I here? What's wrong?" Here again, no one needs to be assigned such questions. In fact, no one can stop the human heart from asking them. Part of children's effort to assemble a complete picture of the world in which they live includes finding answers to such questions.

IS EVERY ANSWER EQUALLY VALID? THE ANSWERS CHILDREN SEEK

When I am speaking with prospective parents at my school about the education we provide, I often ask, "How do you like my pink tie?" when my tie is quite evidently another color. When they politely say, "It is a great tie, Tom, but it isn't pink," I say, "Well, for you it is blue, but for me it is pink." My point is that children do not create their own reality. And the goal of schooling is to help children understand the nature of reality. Another word for something that corresponds to reality is *truth*; if something is true, it reflects the way things really are. To be human is to seek to find answers to questions about the world in which we live, and the answers we seek are the truth; they correspond to the way things really are.

It is quite easy to illustrate the wrong thinking about the nature of reality when you can see that my blue tie is not actually, in truth, pink. But what about the nature of truth and reality not seen by the eyes or unable to be verified by the methods of science? Is every idea equally valid in these cases? Are children able to create their own realities here? Or, returning to our image of puzzle assembly, does every piece of data children receive fit the puzzle of the truth about the world they are assembling? No. There is truth beyond what we see as well. The human mind and heart seek to understand the nature of all created realities, and the answers we seek to the questions we are asking will correspond to the truth or the way things really are.

These important ideas—the types of questions all humans seek to answer and the desire for answers to correspond to reality—will be critical as we explore why the selection of a child's school is an important decision.

Parents and caregivers have the right to select the kind of schooling their child will receive and their ability to choose a school is meaningful only if there are different options from which to choose. Baskin-Robbins ice cream stores made their reputation by advertising thirty-one flavors of ice cream from which to choose. If I walked into a Baskin-Robbins and found the thirty-one flavors were all variations of vanilla, my ability to choose would mean very little to me. But that is not the case, as the flavors vary widely. Some flavors I might find very distasteful. I think of the ice cream stand in Colorado that is purported to serve Goat Cheese Beet Swirl. No thanks. Others I find consistent with my idea of great ice cream, like Ben and Jerry's Chunky Monkey. Yum!

Some parents view the choice of their children's school similar to choosing from among variations of vanilla. I mean, are they not all pretty similar with some subtle variations? I will argue the choice is more similar to choosing between Goat Cheese Beet Swirl and Chunky Monkey than among variations of vanilla. Read on to see what I mean.

A MASSIVE DISTINCTION AMONG SCHOOLS: THE VISION FOR HUMAN FLOURISHING

The single most significant ingredient that differentiates Christian schooling from other types of schools is what the people in Christian schools believe is essential for children to flourish in their lives and be all they are capable of being. This vision for human flourishing pervades all aspects of the mission of Christian schooling. It is also consistent with an extraordinarily long history in education—back all the way to the earliest idea of schools among the ancient Greeks—that acknowledges that knowledge and virtue cannot be separated. Why? Because the cultivation of the mind is inextricably bound to the cultivation of the heart or character. Precisely because of the role education plays in helping students assemble a complete picture of the world that includes answers to the most important questions on students' minds, we arrive at a foundational conclusion about education in any school, best captured by a dear friend and my doctoral adviser at Boston University in these words: "Real *education* is never neutral because real education always rests upon an understanding of what is required for human beings to flourish, to be all they are capable of being. And that involves making choices among competing visions."[1]

This idea is essential as we explore what makes a Christian school so valuable for students. Let's begin to explore it more deeply by defining what it means for children to flourish in their lives.

WHAT DOES IT MEAN FOR HUMAN BEINGS TO FLOURISH?

If we intend to define the goal of education as human flourishing or help-ing students become all they are capable of being, here it will be helpful to provide a clearer picture of what we mean. What does human flourishing look like? As you think about your own life or the life of your child or grandchild, what do you believe is characteristic of the good life? This is an important question and a good example of an idea worthy of a book of its own. Volumes have been written with the singular goal of defining what it means for human beings to flourish. For the purpose of this primer, however, I propose three aspects essential to any definition.

The first entails abundance, completeness, wholeness, health, and vi-tality. A flourishing life is the opposite of merely eking out an existence. This is captured well throughout Scripture in places such as Jesus's "I have come that they may have life, and have it to the full" (John 10:10) and in Psalm 1, extolling the person who "is like a tree planted by streams of water, which yields its fruit in season and whose leaf does not wither—whatever they do prospers." Other powerful ideas capture this same aspect, including the Hebrew concept of shalom, often defined with ideas such as peace or harmony, the biblical idea of wisdom, and the philosophic idea of the *sum-mum bonum* or "highest good" first popularized by the Roman philosopher Cicero in the first century BC. The same idea is captured in contemporary culture in conceptions of "the good life" and a "life well lived." To flourish is to thrive and be fully alive.

A second essential characteristic is that human flourishing acknowl-edges a fixed intentionally designed destination. Therefore, a flourishing life is marked by movement in the direction of this predetermined destina-tion. This characteristic of human flourishing flies in the face of the com-mon idea that the good life is what you make it to be. The good life, rather, is what God designed and intended it to be. This is the overarching theme of all of Scripture. The living God creates the world and declares it good. The fall of humankind distorted the goodness of this intention, but all of Scripture recounts God's plan of redemption by which all of creation can and will be restored to God's original intention. The Westminster Shorter Catechism captures the same idea in question 1: "What is the chief end of man?" with the answer, "To glorify God, and to enjoy him forever." The point is that there is an end to which we were designed. The same idea of a fixed destination intentionally designed is captured in Plato's famous cave analogy, which depicts people in chains in the cave looking at shadows of images against the wall. According to Plato, the process of education frees the people from their chains and enables them to turn and climb out of the cave to behold reality in the light of the sun. The fixed destination has implications for all of life, including work, family, faith, and character.

I was tempted to make the third aspect of my proposed definition of human flourishing implicit to the first idea of abundance, but it is important enough to warrant a place of its own. A life of human flourishing is marked by internal peace, harmony, and happiness that is inextricably bound to a deepening awareness of and relationship with the living God who is loving and good. In a world filled with rampant angst-anxiety, the promise of a path toward personal peace, gladness, and deep satisfaction has greater meaning. The theme of peace through a restored relationship with God is woven throughout Scripture and reflected again in the Westminster Catechism's answer to the question about the chief end of man—"to glorify God, and to enjoy him forever." These three aspects combine in a definition of human flourishing as the *gracious reward of living in a way consistent with God's good and loving design*. I propose that this is what Christian parents desire for their children, and Christian schools are uniquely poised to educate children in a way that aligns with this clearly defined target.

A NEUTRAL EDUCATION IS IMPOSSIBLE

Many people have believed an idea that turns out to be impossible. Namely, that students can be instructed in facts and knowledge about the world separate from or unattached to any value judgement about what is right and wrong or input about what is necessary for a child to flourish. This belief is perfectly understandable because many school subjects seem quite neutral or absent any value judgment that could be considered even remotely controversial. So, 2 + 2 = 4, the capital of Massachusetts is Boston, cells divide in a process called mitosis. How are these ideas highly charged or laden with values? We can all think of elements in the content of schooling that are quite neutral in the same way we can all think of elements that are highly controversial. It will be worth taking a closer look at the various ways values permeate a student's experience at school.

THE POWER OF CONTENT AND ASSESSMENT

We have defined real education as extending beyond the transferring of factual information from teachers to students because it is impossible to deliver this content apart from a conception of human flourishing as defined by the beliefs, ideas, attitudes, and actions that are to be *valued* above other alternatives.[2] When a teacher reads a story to young students or leads a discussion on a novel, students think about the actions of the characters, observe their impact, and evaluate the consequences the characters experience for their actions. This routine practice contributes to the child's understanding of what is good or bad and right or wrong, and it is repeated many times each day in every subject. In history class, students consider the foundational ideas that motivated individuals or groups to take actions that often had wide-ranging consequences upon individuals or society as a whole.

Although it may be easier to illustrate values in the school subjects that study the human experience, the shaping of students' values is not limited to these areas. In the hard sciences, students learn how and why math, science, and technology work, even as they confront the implications of challenging, value-laden questions: how can each be used for great benefit or serious harm, for good or for evil, to people and society?

The people who write textbooks and tests must make value judgments regarding what particular content to include and exclude and the particular perspectives from which the texts will be written. For instance, most science textbooks reflect the perspective of atheistic naturalism and frame the study of the field according to the theory of human evolution. Most history texts reflect a progressive ideological viewpoint and frame the study of the field through the lens of ideas consistent with this perspective. The reigning ideas in each field pervade the content of the subject or course and often are reflected in the assessments created to evaluate student learning. Whether the assessments are created by a classroom teacher for an individual class or by the government or other nationwide agency, the tests students take require them to demonstrate more than a grasp of objectively sterile or neutral facts and often reward student responses that align with the perspectives of the person or people who wrote the test.

The College Board's 2014 revisions of the framework for teaching Advanced Placement United States History (APUSH) clearly reflect how writers make value judgments about the content taught to students. The APUSH course is very popular in high schools, taken by more than five hundred thousand college-bound students each year. The 2014 revisions received widespread criticism, especially from scholars in the field of history, charging that the new frameworks presented a particular interpretation of American history reflecting political and ideological biases, including a clear anti-America theme.[3]

This biased perspective would be taught to AP students with the reasonable expectation that students reflect it in their responses on the AP exams. In the face of stiffening opposition, the College Board repealed its revisions and presented new course frameworks—but not before providing a clear example of how the value judgments of others shape the content of education, which then influences students' understanding of what is true, right, and good.

Given some of the highly charged issues of race, gender, sexuality, and political ideologies in our culture today, similar examples may come to mind of the ways particular values and biases, whether overt or subtle, may be presented in the academic content in school.

THE POWER OF SCHOOL CONTEXT

The particular school *context* in which learning takes place is equally influential to the specific academic content. An individual school, a school district, or even national policies regarding the beliefs, attitudes, and actions that it celebrates and disciplines reflect the values it wishes to engender in its students. Teachers also establish the policies by which the classroom will be managed, reflecting the values the teacher wishes to engender in the students. However, the relationships students have at school influence them the most. This includes students with teachers, students with coaches and directors, students with administrators, counselors, and all school personnel. The context of these relationships is life shaping because it involves instruction in a particular subject, sport, or activity while modeling—for the students' benefit or harm, intentionally or unintentionally, by example or instruction—the administration's beliefs and values about what is required for students to flourish. Finally, the context of education includes the very influential relationships students have with other students. The peer culture exerts extraordinary power on students' beliefs, attitudes, and actions, causing adults to marvel at times at the decisions made when influenced by even one but especially a group of peers. If we take all of these and add them together, we see clearly why Vryhof writes: "Values permeate all of schooling—curriculum, structures, policies, pedagogy, assessment—and all types of relationships. And the adult-child relationships of schooling— such as teacher to student, coach to student, counselor to student—provide the nurture, support, and modeling so crucial to shaping the child."[4]

CONCEPTIONS OF HUMAN FLOURISHING

The important question is what foundational system of values does a particular school teach; what particular vision is upheld to show a child how to flourish and be all he or she is capable of being? Perhaps more accurately, what *conceptions* of human flourishing is the child receiving from textbooks, assessments, school policies, teachers, coaches, and peers? These voices often speak in conflict with one another, and these conflicting and unclear messages about what is true, right, and good can confuse the child who is attempting to make sense of the world.

Returning to our illustration of children assembling the constant stream of puzzle pieces into a complete picture of the world and life: If it were possible to provide a value-neutral education in any school context, parents or caregivers might believe the puzzle pieces their children are receiving will fit into the picture each child is creating but merely be limited to a more mundane or less important aspect of the picture. Content to get these pieces of the puzzle from the school, parents will likely hope the children fill out the picture with pieces they receives at home, at church, or from other relationships and organizations that share the family's vision for human flourishing. I suspect this is a common view held by many parents and caregivers today.

The reality of the situation is much different. The values the child is receiving from conflicting conceptions of what is required for humans to flourish are puzzle pieces that actually fit a different picture, one with an alternative and competing vision of what is required for the child to flourish. This stream of puzzle pieces that belong to different pictures undermines a child's efforts to construct a complete picture of the world reflecting the truth of all created realities. Students from Christian families in such school contexts face a challenge to piece together a complete and cohesive understanding of all truth, by bringing together what they learn at school with the convictions of faith and the values rooted in faith they learn at home and in church.

Many students and parents underestimate the formative influence such educational contexts have upon the way they or their children understand and interpret the world. The challenge can certainly be overcome, especially with vigilant and intentional help of the Christian home and the support of an engaged church community. Truth is powerful and the nature of reality has a way of making itself known to the honest seeker. In fact, some highly motivated students, prepared to do the challenging work of bringing together the faith and values taught in their homes and churches with the content and context of their education at school, may be stronger for the experience. But the importance and great challenge of this task highlight the idea of a Christian school and the value of its unified vision of human flourishing consistent with the faith and values of the Christian home.

A FOUNDATIONAL IDEA OF CHRISTIAN SCHOOLING

This brings us to the very foundation of the idea of a Christian school. A Christian school has a unified vision for what is required for students to flourish in their lives and be all they were created to be. This vision is rooted in Christian faith and values, shared by all teachers, coaches, and other school personnel, and intentionally nurtured to give shape to all aspects of both the content and context of the school program, in and outside of the classroom. In Christian schools, teachers and coaches are not only allowed by law to provide intentional instruction from this shared vision of human flourishing, they are required to do so and are provided specialized training to enable them to promote the distinctive nature of the school. This is why Christian schools exist in the private-school marketplace, and it is key to the life-shaping value they provide students and their families. This is also what makes a Christian school so distinctive—a flavor more similar to Goat Cheese Beet Swirl or Chunky Monkey than merely a variation of vanilla.

Parents and caregivers have the right, and privilege, to select a school that educates children in a manner consistent with their identity and values as shaped by their personal beliefs about human flourishing—beliefs often rooted in the convictions of religious faith. In the United States, there are more than thirty thousand private schools enrolling more than 5 million students. Approximately 70 percent of the private schools have a religious orientation and purpose; these schools enroll 80 percent—more than 3.5

million—of the students in private schools. In addition, more than 3 million students are homeschooled.[5]

Research studies consistently support the logical and intuitive notion that the most significant reason parents give for choosing to homeschool or send their children to private Christian schools is their desire to have their children educated in a school that shares their vision of human flourishing rooted in the convictions of Christian faith.

SUMMARY

The Idea of a Christian School starts by recognizing that education is one of the most powerful life-shaping influences in a child's life. To be human means to seek to assemble a complete picture of the world and the truth about all created realities. Schooling is a big part of this process, and a long-standing tradition holds that the cultivation of the mind is inextricably bound to the cultivation of the heart. A major thesis of this book, and a foundational truth for Christian schooling, is that real education always rests upon an understanding of what is required for human beings to flourish and be all they are capable of being. There is no such thing as a values-neutral education, as values permeate both the content and context of a child's education from sources such as textbooks, school policies and procedures, individual teachers and other personnel, and peers. The important question is not "if" a child is exposed to values, but, rather, in what system of values and particular vision of human flourishing is a child's education rooted? The children of parents and caregivers whose vision of human flourishing is rooted in Christian faith receive wide-ranging and often conflicting messages about what is right and true in public schools and private non-faith-based schools. These messages make it more challenging for children to assemble a complete and cohesive understanding of the world. This is why Christian schools exist in the marketplace of schools and why parents have the right and privilege to select a school that educates children in a manner consistent with their identity, values, and beliefs about human flourishing.

In the next chapter, we will look more closely at the components of the shared vision of human flourishing in Christian schools and why they hold such power to shape students' minds and hearts.

2

The Unity of All Truth

Helping Children Assemble a Complete Picture of the World

"The idea of a Christian school is its mission to educate students in a way that brings together the study of the truth of God's world in the academic disciplines with the truth of God's Word to provide students with a complete and cohesive view of the world in which they live."

—Tom Stoner

"I believe in Christianity as I believe the sun has risen: not only because I see it, but because by it I see everything else."

—C. S. Lewis

The Christian school is founded upon the belief that there is a true and living God who has revealed himself in the world he created and also in his Word—the written Word of the Bible and the "Word made flesh" in the person of Jesus Christ. This belief is presupposed to be true, rooted as it is in the convictions of the historic Christian faith. As I write, I am reminded of a professor in my seminary training who told us not to give up the truth of God and the Bible and try to argue our way to prove both are true. Rather, he said, begin with the truth of God and the Bible then show anyone who will listen how it all fits together in a satisfying and comprehensive view of reality. This is the place where Christian schools begin.

WHAT EXACTLY DO I MEAN BY "CHRISTIAN SCHOOLS"? CATHOLIC SCHOOLS? COLLEGES?

It is important to identify at this point what I mean by the terms *Christian* and *school*. Am I talking about Catholic schools? How about Lutheran schools? And am I talking about elementary schools only, or do I include high schools and colleges? In my work in Christian schooling over the years, I have found it common for people to view Christian schools and Catholic schools in two different categories. I have learned to clarify for prospective parents that I use the term *Christian* at the highest level to identify our belief in Jesus Christ and to differentiate from other religions such as Buddhism or Islam. Viewed this way, Catholic schools are certainly Christian. Within the Christian faith (or on the next level down from the term *Christian*), there are the two major divisions of Catholic and Protestant. Within each of these there are the various Catholic orders and Protestant denominations. There are many shared beliefs and some very real differences among the many types of Christian schools, and I will touch on these beliefs and differences throughout this book. In short, I use the term *Christian* to include any school that takes as its starting place the triune God of creation, revealed in the Bible, and in the person of Jesus Christ.

Similarly, I use the term *schools* at the highest, most general level to refer to any school or any type of educational organization designed to teach students to better understand the world in which they live. I have spent my career working in primary and secondary schools (K–12), but the ideas presented here apply directly to colleges and universities as well. One of the aims of this book is to better prepare parents, grandparents, teachers, and all school leaders to identify the extent to which any particular school incorporates these ideas into the warp and woof of its daily operation.

KNOWING GOD THROUGH CREATION, HIS WORD, AND THE PERSON OF JESUS CHRIST

In the first sentence of the Old Testament, we read the familiar words, "In the beginning God created the heavens and the earth." The "heavens and the earth" combine to represent everything God created—all that is seen and all that is unseen. In the New Testament, the apostle Paul echoes these same words, describing the supremacy of Jesus Christ: "The Son is the image of the invisible God, the firstborn over all creation. For in him all things were created: *things in heaven and on earth*, visible and invisible, whether thrones or powers or rulers or authorities; all things have been created through him and for him" (Colossians 1:15–17, italics added). All created realities find their source in the living God who spoke them into existence to display his power and to share the glory of his character.

I chose the phrase "all created *realities*" intentionally because the goal of education is to teach students to understand the truth about the world in which they live. We have already identified a very practical definition of truth as corresponding to reality. If something is true, it reflects what is real or the way things really are. The writers of Scripture consistently affirm these two realms of truth in the universe. The first is truth revealed in the visible creation. The first verses of Psalm 19, attributed to David, are among the texts most often cited by people writing on the philosophy of Christian schooling:

> The heavens declare the glory of God;
> the skies proclaim the work of his hands.
> Day after day they pour forth speech;
> night after night they reveal knowledge.
> They have no speech, they use no words;
> no sound is heard from them.
> Yet their voice goes out into all the earth,
> their words to the ends of the world.[6]

The study of the academic disciplines in school is primarily the study of the truth of the world God made.

The second realm of truth is God's Word, the Bible—the Scriptures of the Old and New Testaments. Scripture testifies in many places to God as the source of the Bible as he inspired the individual authors to write. The most familiar text is the words of the apostle Paul to his young disciple, Timothy, "All Scripture is God-breathed" and Jesus's own words in his prayer for his disciples before he was crucified: "Sanctify them by the truth; your word is truth." In addition to the words of God written in the pages of Scripture, the prologue of John's Gospel describes Jesus Christ as the human Word—the visible expression of God's truth: "The Word became flesh and made his dwelling among us," a fact that Jesus affirmed by saying, "I am the way and the truth and the life."[7] The truth found in the creation God has made and the truth of God's Word—in Scripture and in Christ—combine to reflect the truth of all created realities. These are the major domains from which our children will draw as they assemble a complete understanding of the world in which they live.

GENERAL AND SPECIAL REVELATION

Theologians and Bible teachers use the terms *general revelation* for God's revelation of himself in the created universe, and *special revelation* for God's revelation of himself in the words of Scripture and the person of Jesus Christ. Throughout history there have been a number of confessions or summaries of the teachings of Scripture. One of them, The Belgic Confession of 1561, describes these realms as two books: God has set the universe "before our eyes like a beautiful book, in which all creatures, great and small, are as letters to make us ponder the invisible things of God" and has made himself known "more clearly by his holy and divine Word, as much as we need in this life, for God's glory and for our salvation."[8]

From the time they are young, students begin to learn the content of the academic disciplines that correspond to the way things really are in the created world around them. They learn that $2 + 2 = 4$ and how the properties of numbers work in mathematics. Students learn the principles of good health and how to throw, catch, and run skillfully in physical education. In chemistry, students learn that all matter is composed of atoms that form bonds to create different compounds. They learn how the laws of physics govern the properties of energy and motion, and so on. The information taught to students in each academic discipline reflects the truth people throughout history have discovered through the study of creation and the lessons of human experience. The graphic below illustrates the dimension of truth and reality taught in the academic disciplines from the study of the created world.

Creator God
Source of All Realities

↓

Truth
Corresponds to Reality

↓

Truth of God's World
General Revelation

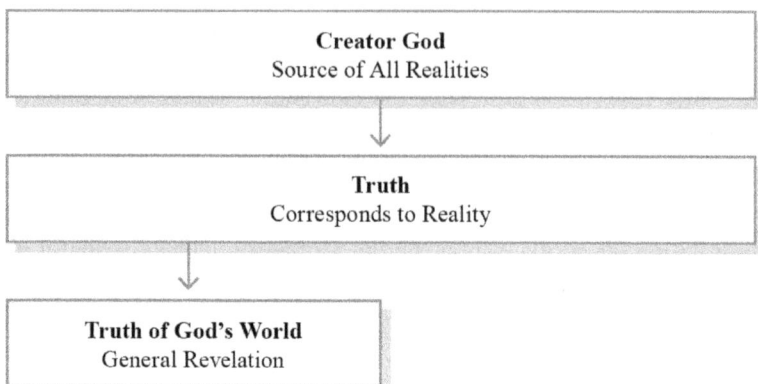

The Truth of God's World

The other dimension of God's truth is not fully visible in the study of the physical world. God has revealed the truth of this dimension of reality in his Word—the Bible. In the pages of Scripture, God provides us with essential elements for human flourishing that simply cannot be found in the study of creation alone; these elements include the meaning and purpose of life, his intention for people to be all he created them to be, and how that is found in relationship with him. The idea of a Christian school is its mission to educate students in a way that brings together the study of the truth of God's world in the academic disciplines with the truth of God's Word to help them assemble a complete and cohesive view of the world in which they live.

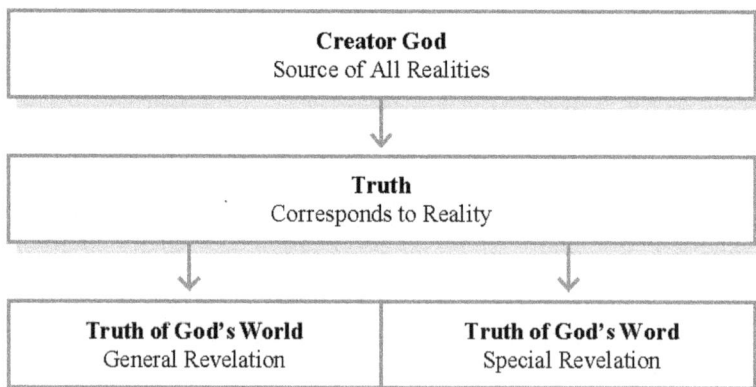

Creator God
Source of All Realities

↓

Truth
Corresponds to Reality

↓ ↓

| **Truth of God's World** | **Truth of God's Word** |
| General Revelation | Special Revelation |

Two Dimensions of Truth and Reality

ALL TRUTH IS GOD'S TRUTH

If God is the source of all created realities and the author of both the book of creation and the book of his Word, and if truth corresponds to reality, then God is the author of all truth. *All truth is God's truth* is a phrase that has become synonymous with Christian schooling. The phrase is sometimes attributed to Frank Gaebelein, the founding headmaster of the Stony Brook School on Long Island, who used it in his highly influential book *The Pattern of Truth* (1954).[9] However, Gaebelein's pithy expression is an echo of earlier Christian voices, including Justin Martyr, the second-century church father, and St. Augustine, who in the fourth century wrote, "Every good and true Christian must recognize that wherever he may find truth, it is the Lord's."[10] When students learn about the created universe, they are studying Christ—the very work of his hands—and through it, they are able to see glimpses of who he is, his power, and reflections of the glory of his character. Abraham Kuyper famously made this same point at the dedication of the Free University of Amsterdam: "There is not a square inch in the whole domain of our human existence over which Christ, who is sovereign over all, does not cry: 'Mine!'"[11]

A SACRED-SECULAR DIVIDE?

An important question related to the idea of Christian schooling is, how does the study of creation relate to the truth revealed in Christ and in his Word? Some people fall into a common trap that views the truth we understand by studying creation to be different, less true, or of a lesser quality than the truth we find revealed in God's Word. Some even describe truth discovered in the created world as "secular," "mundane,"[12] or even "worldly" and the truth revealed in the Bible as "spiritual" or "sacred." But the purpose of schooling is to contribute to our students' efforts to assemble a complete picture of all truth—all created realities, and, to this end, all truth is of the same nature and finds its source in God. Frank Gaebelein warned of this in 1954:

> It is perfectly possible to recognize the diverse importance of different aspects of truth without in any way denying its indissoluble nature. We do indeed give the primacy to that spiritual truth revealed in the Bible and incarnate in Christ. That does not mean, however, that those aspects of truth discoverable by man in the

realm of mathematics, chemistry, or geography, are any whit less God's truth than the truth as it is in Christ.[13]

This brings us to two important conclusions for the idea of Christian schooling that we add to the common mantra "all truth is God's truth." Now we also conclude that "truth is truth." Whether found in the study of created things or revealed in the Bible, the truth of both is of the same nature. The second new conclusion is that the truth of both dimensions combine to form a complete, cohesive unity of all truth. The goal of Christian schooling is for students to understand this complete and unified picture of the world.

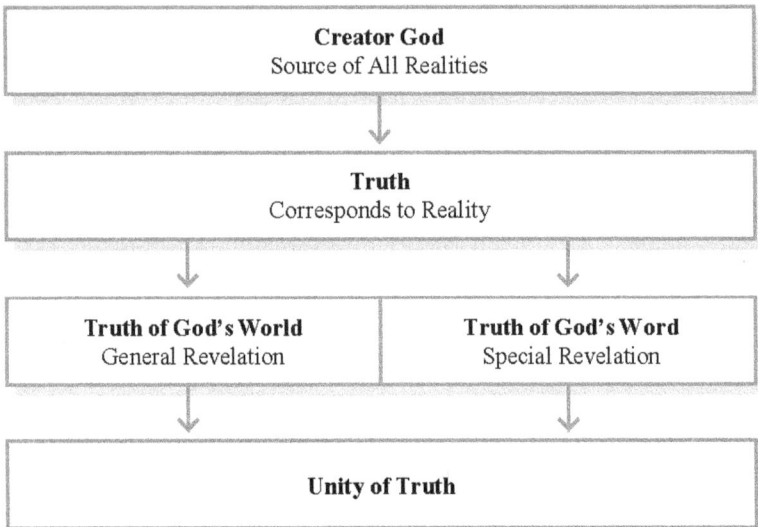

```
┌─────────────────────────────────────────┐
│            Creator God                   │
│        Source of All Realities           │
└─────────────────────────────────────────┘
                    ↓
┌─────────────────────────────────────────┐
│              Truth                       │
│        Corresponds to Reality            │
└─────────────────────────────────────────┘
         ↓                      ↓
┌──────────────────┬──────────────────────┐
│ Truth of God's World │ Truth of God's Word │
│ General Revelation   │ Special Revelation  │
└──────────────────┴──────────────────────┘
         ↓                      ↓
┌─────────────────────────────────────────┐
│            Unity of Truth                │
└─────────────────────────────────────────┘
```

The Unified Nature of All Truth

WHAT DIFFERENCE WILL A UNIFIED UNDERSTANDING OF TRUTH MAKE FOR MY CHILD?

As children seek to understand the world in which they live, learning in a way that brings together the truth of God's world and the truth of God's word into a unity of truth helps them construct a complete and cohesive picture of the world. It is complete because truth from each dimension combines to provide answers to all the questions their minds seek to answer. It is also cohesive because the truth from each dimension combines to provide a picture that fits together in one unified image of the world. This ability to assemble a complete and cohesive picture of the world is foundational to human flourishing.

The unified nature of truth does not mean the content of the truth of creation and the content of the truth of Scripture are equally important. Failing to understand the truth of math, physical education, biology, music, and so forth can certainly have consequences, some of which may be serious. But to be mistaken about God's intention for human flourishing at creation and his plan for restoring creation from the effects of the fall through the person and work of Jesus Christ has consequences that extend beyond this life to the next.

The error of constructing an artificial sacred-versus-secular divide between the truth of God's world and the truth of God's Word, and relegating the truth discovered in the study of creation to a second-class status, will undermine the unity of truth by devaluing the study of the academic disciplines and attempting to find information in the Bible it may not be intending to speak to. We will explore the challenges these pose to the mission of Christian schooling in later chapters.

I observed a rather extreme example of parents devaluing the truth found in the study of creation and human experience. A middle-school boy was expressing anger in violent drawings and occasional threatening verbal outbursts. We brought the problem to the attention of his parents, fine people—his dad was the pastor of local congregation. The anger problems escalated and presented concerns for the safety of the boy himself and those around him. We eventually required a psychological evaluation as a condition for his ongoing enrollment. We were shocked when the father told us, "We don't believe in psychology. The Bible is all we need in order to deal with this issue. If you are going to require an appointment with a psychologist, then we will pull him out of school." And that is precisely what they did. In this situation the parents did more than discount the value of what psychologists have discovered in more than a century of intentional study of the impact of life experiences upon the human person; they completely rejected it as invalid. In so doing, they denied themselves and their child the value of the truth of psychology regarding the source of anger and methods available to help resolve the problem so the student could better flourish.

All truth is God's truth! Whether students are studying music, math, physics, or Bible, all truth finds its source in God's world and God's Word.

Truth is truth! The truth of God's world and God's Word reflect the way things are in each dimension; therefore they are both of the same nature, truth. Truth is unified! The truth of both dimensions combine together to form a complete, cohesive unity of all truth. As we consider the mission of Christian schooling to help students understand all truth, it is important to identify the different tools we use to grasp the truth of each dimension.

THE TOOLS NEEDED TO UNDERSTAND THE TRUTH OF BOTH DIMENSIONS

Students understand the truth of creation by means of the human capacity of reason or the ability to think rationally, inquire, analyze, deduce, and form conclusions about the world around them. This extraordinary ability is a fundamental and distinguishing mark of what it means for all people to be created in the image of God.[14] By the power of reason, the human race has invented, discovered, and accomplished many wonders of human achievement and the expansion of knowledge about the created universe that continues at an astounding pace. I immediately think of the pyramids of Egypt, Solomon's temple in Jerusalem, Plato's *Republic*, the invention of the lightbulb, Jonas Salk and all of modern medicine, the Sistine Chapel, the Wright Brothers' mastery of human flight, Handel's *Messiah*, the Taj Mahal, the moon landing, the discovery of the double-helix structure of DNA and ultimately to the Human Genome Project, and the Library of Congress. It is the power of human reason that produced these wonders, a God-given capacity that is essential to fulfill what theologians refer to as the "cultural mandate" of Genesis 1:28, where Adam and Eve are told to "Be fruitful and increase in number; *fill the earth and subdue it*. Rule over the fish in the sea and the birds in the sky and over every living creature that moves on the ground."[15]

LIMITS TO REASON

Despite the triumphs of human reason, the fall of humankind has made it impossible for unaided reason to understand the whole dimension of truth and reality revealed in God's Word and the person of Jesus Christ. Understanding the truth of this dimension requires the light of Christian faith.

Our ability to understand the world by means of the human capacity to reason alone is similar to our ability to see with our eyes at night. Our eyes have the ability to use the light of nature to see clearly some things in the world around us. But much of what we see appears as mere shadows of the realities themselves; still more of the world is entirely hidden from our view—our eyes being limited in their ability. This limitation alone would be enough of a challenge, but the problem is worse yet. The fall of humanity in the garden of Eden has also impacted this God-given capacity, making us inclined to see in distorted and inaccurate ways. The addition of Christian faith, or belief, to our natural ability to reason is similar to a powerful new source of light. The new light makes it possible to see more clearly what had appeared to us only as shadows. It enables our eyes to see the realities that had been completely hidden in darkness and see more accurately what had been distorted. Faith always comes before understanding the dimension of reality revealed in the Bible. "By faith we understand that the universe was formed at God's command, so that what is seen was not made out of what was visible" (Hebrews 11:3). It is impossible for people to reason their way into this, not because the truth we understand by faith is irrational or contrary to reason, but because the door through which this understanding is accessed is never reason alone; it is reason informed by Christian faith. Christian educators, theologians, and writers throughout history have recognized that faith precedes a complete understanding of all truth. St. Augustine's words, latter attributed to St. Anselm, have become a maxim of Catholic education: "I believe in order that I might understand." C. S. Lewis expressed the same truth this way: "I believe in Christianity as I believe that the Sun has risen, not only because I see it, but because by it I see everything else."[16]

To help students understand the relationship between faith and reason, I gave my seventh- and eighth-grade Bible classes an assignment to identify statements that are (1) rational or aligned with reason, (2) irrational or contrary to reason, and (3) nonrational,[17] meaning neither simply aligned with reason nor contrary to it. "It is dark and cloudy today; I think I'll take my umbrella" is a rational statement. "If you loved me, you would let me do whatever I want" is an irrational statement often spoken by adolescent children to their parents. "On the third day, Christ rose from the dead" is a nonrational statement. It is not rational, because the power of reason alone will never conclude it. The statement is not irrational, because the most reasonable explanation for the empty tomb is the truth: Jesus's body passed through the grave clothes and resurrected in space and time in an unprecedented state of existence. The reasonability of the statement is understood only in the light of Christian faith.

In addition to reason's inability to understand the dimension of truth and reality that is informed by Christian faith, reason alone is also power-less to change the condition of the human heart after the effect of the fall in the garden of Eden. The sin of human pride has distorted our thoughts and actions in ways contrary to God's intention at creation. It has corrupted our affections away from loving God and that which is true, beautiful, and just. Instead we are drawn to loving the world, described by the apostle John as "the lust of the flesh, the lust of the eyes, and the pride of life" (1 John 2:16). The natural condition of our hearts not only limits our ability to know all truth, but also hinders our ability to carry it out.

In his book *The Idea of a University*, Catholic educator John Henry Newman identified the impotence of knowledge and reason to overcome these obstacles. Newman affirmed that human flourishing ultimately in-volves slaying giants—"passion and pride"—present in the human heart. These giants are the inheritance of all people, everywhere, traced in our lineage back to our first human parents. How does one slay these giants? Newman compared the use of "knowledge and human reason" alone to someone quarrying "granite rock with razors" or mooring a "vessel with a thread of silk."[18]

These limitations of human reason alone have important implications as we seek to educate students to flourish and become all they were cre-ated to be. We are drawn back to the long-standing tradition in education, that (1) knowledge and virtue are interdependent and (2) the cultivation of minds is inextricably bound to the cultivation of hearts. Reason alone will not construct the complete picture of all truth we long for children to understand or heal the deepest needs of their hearts.

THE ADDITION OF CHRISTIAN FAITH

The Bible uses the same imagery of light and darkness to describe the im-pact the fall has had on our minds and hearts by saying that all people are born "darkened in their understanding" and "futile in their thinking" because of the "ignorance that is in them" due to the "hardening of their hearts" and the "darkness in their foolish hearts."[19] Because of our clouded understanding and futile thinking, we do not understand the truth revealed in God's Word, and the hardness and foolishness of our hearts make us unwilling and unable to carry it out. Education for human flourishing requires changed minds and changed hearts from a source outside of our natural abilities.

The Bible uses the term *new birth* and theologians the term *conversion* to describe the transformation that begins when God's Spirit brings new life to a person's heart. The first verse of the famous hymn "Amazing Grace," written by former slave trader John Newton, illustrates his dramatic change of heart and conversion to Christian faith:

> Amazing Grace, how sweet the sound
> that saved a wretch like me.
> I once was lost, but now am found,
> was blind but now I see.

Throughout the New Testament, we read the language of conversion from darkness to light and the effect of the Holy Spirit's power and presence in the human heart:

> Jesus replied, "Very truly I tell you, no one can see the kingdom of God unless they are born again." (John 3:3)

> The person without the Spirit does not accept the things that come from the Spirit of God but considers them foolishness, and cannot understand them because they are discerned only through the Spirit. (1 Corinthians 2:14)

> But when he, the Spirit of Truth, comes, he will guide you into all the truth. (John 16:13)

> For you were once darkness, but now you are light in the Lord. Live as children of light (for the fruit of the light consists in all goodness, righteousness, and truth) and find out what pleases the Lord. (Ephesians 5:8–10)

The power of the Holy Spirit results in personal faith and life changes that extend beyond the limitations of human reason. Faith from the Spirit begins the process of renewing our minds by bringing the light of new understanding to areas of truth that were previously in darkness or distorted by the impact of the fall. The Spirit also brings a new power to our hearts, enabling us to begin to live differently not only by doing what is morally and ethically right and good, but by doing so with new affections of love for God, love for others, and love for what is true, right, and good. The work of the Spirit in conversion begins the lifelong process of what the apostle Paul refers to as sanctification. This is the life of human flourishing God intended for us at creation and by which we become in truth all he created us to be.

IMPLICATIONS FOR CHRISTIAN SCHOOLING

A foundational tenet of Christian schooling is its ability, in fact its very mission, to educate students to understand both books—the book of creation and the book of God's Word, using both tools—human reason together with Christian faith—to help students understand a complete and cohesive view of the world in which they live.

It is important to note that faith does not generate new knowledge about the universe but is simply an openness to what is already revealed[20] or the means by which students are able to understand the dimension of truth and reality that is revealed in the words of Scripture and in the person of Jesus Christ. The inclusion of faith in instruction by Christian teachers enables students to begin to understand the world in a way that includes the dimension of truth and reality which is hidden, or out of view to the powers of natural reason alone. In this way, education from a perspective of Christian faith is expansive, for it provides students with a firm place to stand from which they are able to explore the additional dimension of truth understood by faith. From this place students are able to view all created realities and construct a complete and cohesive view of the world.[21]

The beginning place for providing students with a complete view of reality is schooling that accepts and includes the revelation of God in the Bible and the person of Jesus Christ, and brings this dimension of truth together with the study of creation in the academic disciplines.

```
┌─────────────────────────────────────────────────┐
│                  Creator God                     │
│             Source of All Realities              │
└─────────────────────────────────────────────────┘
                        │
                        ▼
┌─────────────────────────────────────────────────┐
│                     Truth                        │
│             Corresponds to Reality               │
└─────────────────────────────────────────────────┘
            │                        │
            ▼                        ▼
┌───────────────────────┐ ┌───────────────────────┐
│  Truth of God's World │ │  Truth of God's Word  │
│ Discovered in Creation│ │  Revealed in Scripture│
│  Understood by Reason │ │Understood by Faith & Reason│
└───────────────────────┘ └───────────────────────┘
            │                        │
            ▼                        ▼
┌─────────────────────────────────────────────────┐
│                 Unity of Truth                   │
└─────────────────────────────────────────────────┘
```

The Unity of All Truth

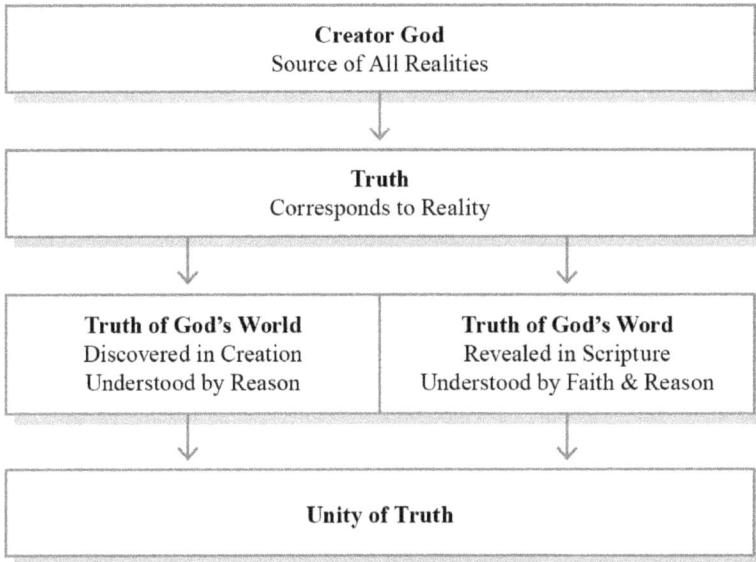

SUMMARY

The idea of Christian schooling begins with the presupposition of a living God who has revealed himself in the world he has made and in his Word—the written words of Scripture and the living Word, Jesus Christ. These are the "two books" through which the world is known. Because God is the source of all created realities and truth corresponds to reality, *all truth is God's truth*. Both realms of truth combine in a unity of truth that provides students with a complete and cohesive picture of the world in which they live; the great advantage of Christian schooling is its ability to provide students with a unified vision of human flourishing. The tools students use to understand truth are reason and reason informed by Christian faith. The addition of faith through a student's new birth or through the instruction by Christian teachers enables students to understand the truth that lies hidden to unaided reason. The combination of faith and reason together enables students to cultivate a complete view of all created realities, and personal faith begins the Spirit's work of transforming a student's heart resulting in love for God and others.

In the next chapter, we will explore more carefully the Christian-school mission to bring together the dimensions of truth and reality and the high privilege and calling of Christian-school teachers to accomplish this task.

3

The Integration of Faith and Learning

What It Is and Why It Matters

"The power of an integrated education is its ability to satisfy the mind's most probing questions and the heart's deepest needs while casting a clear vision for what is required for students to flourish and become all they are capable of being."

—TOM STONER

"The Bible shows the way to go to heaven, not the way the heavens go."

—AUTHOR UNCERTAIN

When I speak with families exploring a Christian school for their children, my job is to help them understand the life-shaping value the school will provide. When it comes to the distinctive value their child will receive because we are a Christian school, parents' minds nearly always go to the addition of Bible class and a weekly chapel service at school. Both are valuable for students. But I go out of my way to help parents see that while their children are studying all of the academic disciplines—literature, science, history, art, music, math—they are encountering ideas, values, and questions informed by what we believe about the meaning of life, what is right and good—ideas related to ethics, morality, and virtue. These ideas and values are rooted in what students believe beyond what is seen, ideas informed by religious faith. In many school contexts, it is illegal for teachers to include such questions in the classroom because of the widely varying belief systems or religions represented among the families. But at a Christian school, it is not only legal to include such ideas, values, and questions in instruction; it is required. It is an enormous benefit to parents to include this dimension of learning in the classroom because it helps children assemble an understanding of the world that is complete and fits together in a cohesive whole. The benefit I am describing to parents is the integration of faith and learning, and it is the hallmark of Christian schooling.

Christian schools exist to present families with an educational choice that enables students to understand the world in a unified, complete, and cohesive way. This takes place over time by providing all instruction, formal and informal, in and out of the classroom, in a way that combines the truth of creation understood through the study of the academic disciplines with the truth revealed in God's Word understood by faith and through the study of Scripture. This bringing together of the historic Christian faith with academics is often called the *integration of faith with learning*. The goal of integrating faith with learning extends far beyond the ability of Christian schools to teach a Bible class and have chapel, far beyond the freedom of Christian-school teachers to open class with prayer and express their personal faith. The mission of Christian schooling calls for a pervasive weaving of Christian faith into the very fabric of learning in all subjects and throughout all the dimensions of life at school. Gaebelein describes the mission this way: "[There is] a vast difference between education in which devotional exercises and the study of Scripture have a place, and education in which the Christianity of the Bible is the matrix of the whole program or, to change the figure, the bed in which the river of teaching and learning flows."[22]

It will help parents, Christian-school educators, and our students to identify some of the challenges to effecting this pervasive integration. We begin by answering some important questions including: Why is truth disintegrated today? What exactly is integration? And how does the content of the Bible relate to the content of the academic disciplines?

DISINTEGRATION IN EDUCATION TODAY

I've heard some peers in Christian schooling say, "I don't like the phrase *integration of faith with learning*, because truth and reality were never dis-integrated in the first place." On one hand, I appreciate this perspective and even agree that reality—the way things are—is not actually separated into the realities visible in creation, addressed in the academic disciplines, and the realities of the invisible creation, understood by faith through God's Word. Both dimensions were the work of God at creation and combine to form a unity of all truth.

On the other hand, the field of education and culture in America in the twenty-first century operate on the basis of an increasingly sharp dualism between these dimensions of reality. Ultimately, teaching the unity of truth requires Christian faith, and today this is possible only in a private Christian school. Why are faith and learning so separate in schools today?

Three fundamentally related factors fuel the operational dualism in American public education. First, America is a pluralist nation and rapidly growing more so. Our public schools serve families and are staffed by personnel with wide-ranging views on what is required for children to flourish and be all they were created to be. Some of these views are rooted in religious beliefs from the five major world religions of Christianity, Buddhism, Islam, Judaism, and Hinduism or from other belief systems, including new age spirituality, paganism, agnosticism, and atheism. Many people point to a time when the values of the Christian home and those promoted in the American public schools were more closely aligned. Some readers no doubt remember saying Christian prayers and singing Christian songs in public schools. But the ever-increasing pluralism in American culture has motivated public schools to target classroom instruction stripped of values traced to any particular belief system, despite this being an impossibility. Values that mirror society as a whole are more evident—particularly self-interest and individual visions of the good life, most often defined in terms of material wealth and status.

The second major force contributing to the operational dualism between truth understood by reason alone and truth understood by Christian faith is the enduring impact of the Enlightenment upon American thought and education. Enlightenment thinking views reason as the most significant capacity for human understanding and exhibits a corresponding suspicion, even outright rejection, of the "blind faith" required by religious faith. The movement began in Europe, vividly expressed in the ideals of the French Revolution, before moving to North America. This period saw great advancement in human knowledge through scientific discovery and by means of the scientific method. The enduring impact of this philosophical thought is to equate knowledge of the material universe alone as objective fact. The realm of religion and anything religion informs—including ethics (that which is right and good) and aesthetics (that which is beautiful and admirable)—is relegated to subjective opinion and personal preference. To Enlightenment thinking, all people are entitled to their own opinions unless what they say can be proven or discounted through scientific experimentation.

The final factor contributing to this operational dualism is the record of Supreme Court decisions interpreting what is known as the Establishment Clause of the First Amendment to the US Constitution—"Congress shall make no law respecting an establishment of religion, or prohibiting the free exercise thereof"—in ways leading to a strict separation between church and state. In the early 1960s, the court made several landmark decisions establishing the current prohibition of state-sponsored prayer in US schools. Now, sixty years later, we see that the high court's decision on prayer was an early indicator of a major shift in American culture. Future court cases, reflected in public policy, would strictly interpret the Establishment Clause, effectively removing from public schools and culture anything and everything that could be linked in any way to religious faith. In a matter of decades, we've gone from having Christian prayer and singing at the start of the public school day to the removal of references to Christmas and debate about removing "under God" from the pledge of allegiance. The historical fact that Christian faith and values played a significant role in the formation of our nation means the shift toward strict separation has been observed and felt more keenly by Christians.

The cumulative and ongoing impact of increasing pluralism, Enlightenment rationalism, and the strictly interpreted separation of church and state has contributed to a complete dis-integration in our public educational system of the truth understood by reason through the study of the academic disciplines and the truth of the historic Christian faith. A direct correspondence to the dis-integration is the promotion of a pervasive worldview best described as *secularism*. This is the world in which we live and the world that welcomes and enfolds our children. The worldview of secularism is reflected throughout the textbooks taught in our K–12 schools and in an overwhelming majority of the universities that train the teachers who instruct our children. This is also the backdrop against which Christian schools attempt to provide an alternative option for families. The mission of Christian schooling is defined by the task of integrating the ideals and values of Christian faith with academic instruction to the end that our children have a complete, cohesive, and unified understanding of all truth.

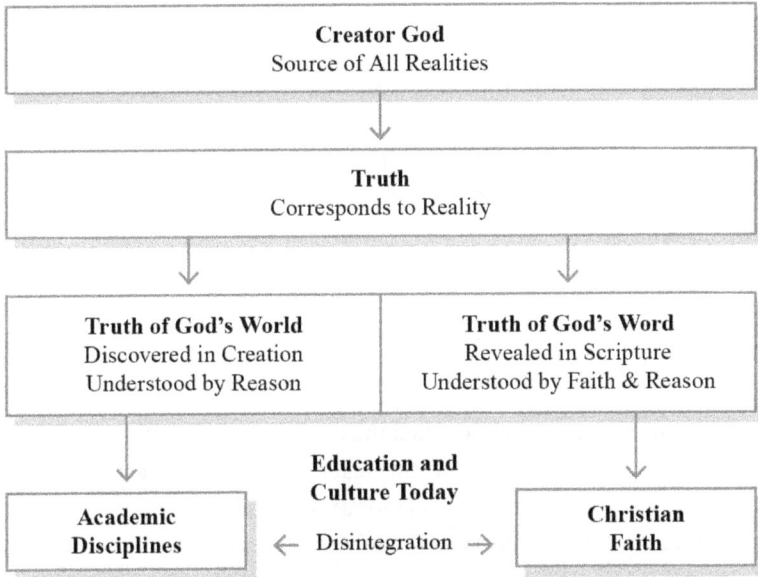

| **Creator God** |
| Source of All Realities |

$\downarrow$

| **Truth** |
| Corresponds to Reality |

$\downarrow$ $\downarrow$

Truth of God's World	**Truth of God's Word**
Discovered in Creation	Revealed in Scripture
Understood by Reason	Understood by Faith & Reason

$\downarrow$ $\downarrow$

Education and Culture Today

| **Academic Disciplines** | $\leftarrow$ Disintegration $\rightarrow$ | **Christian Faith** |

The Reality of Disintegration Today

UNDERSTANDING INTEGRATION

The task of genuinely integrating faith with learning begins with a deeper understanding of what integration is and what we are trying to do in the Christian-school classroom. The most helpful definition I have found is by Robert Harris, who describes integration this way:

> This is the heart of integration. Integration involves the development of interconnections, relationships, and mutual clarifications between Christian truth and academic content. We might call integration the construction—or discovery—of the wholeness and coherence of all knowledge, specifically of the knowledge about human nature and human destiny . . . What is at issue is the relationship, the unification, between what Scripture tells us about the meaning and purpose of life, our origin, the image of God in us,

and the knowledge obtained by research, thinking, discovery, and the study of the natural world and the human person.[23]

Integration is reading Scripture alongside the natural world to identify how the two connect together to form a complete understanding of all truth. This means that *when integration is properly done*, the truth of the Bible is not in conflict with the truth from any source in the natural world. Attempts at integration are often hindered, however, by deeply flawed approaches, rooted in a fundamental misunderstanding of the relationship between the Bible and the natural world. These misunderstandings sometimes have a significant negative impact upon our students' academic preparation and ability to flourish.

THE BIBLE AND ACADEMIC DISCIPLINES: FRIENDS OR FOES?

It will help our students to know that the history of the relationship between the Bible and the conclusions of the academic study of creation has been marked more by conflict than collaboration. One of the clearest examples is that Ptolemy's view of Earth as the center of the universe was understood for centuries to be what the Bible taught in Psalm 104:5: "[God] set the earth on its foundations; it can never be moved." Because of this, Christians initially resisted the Copernican theory that Earth orbits the sun. Those who ascribed to this radical new idea of planet Earth orbiting the sun were branded as heretics. The data Copernicus presented in 1543 from his study of nature was inconsistent with a plain reading of Psalm 104. This example raises the question at hand, how does the Bible relate to the discoveries of science? Is the message of the Bible in the psalm a statement about astronomy and the relationship of the earth to the sun, or is the message of the psalm a statement about theology and the relationship of the creator God to his creation? Gaebelein wrote about this in 1954: "It was not Scripture that was faulty, but the Christian understanding of the Scripture. So also when the church finally admitted to the truth of Copernical astronomy, the Bible was illuminated not overthrown."[24]

Christians misunderstood the message of the psalm as a statement about the movement of the planets. Copernicus's brilliant scientific discovery helped Bible interpreters better understand the intended message of Scripture. Gaebelein (again, he is writing in 1954) also draws an interesting twentieth-century parallel to the Copernican revolution:

In our day, the same principle holds; it is becoming increasingly plain, for example, that man is far older than the traditional 6,000 years. The newest development [from science] that is shedding light on its antiquity is the carbon clock . . . Clearly the traditional ideas of the antiquity of man will have to be revised. But will this change the essential truth of the wonderful Genesis account of creation? Certainly not; on the contrary, it will simply broaden and deepen our understanding of that truth.[25]

Would Gaebelein be surprised and disappointed that, nearly seventy years later, the issue of integrating the interpretation of the Bible with the data of science regarding the age of the universe remains a deeply divisive issue within the Christian faith and one that has significant consequences for the mission of Christian schooling?

The idea, and sometimes the reality in experience, that Scripture and the academic disciplines are foes fighting to occupy the same territory makes the effort to integrate them look more like a hostile takeover than a unification of two complementary dimensions of truth. The challenge of authentic integration is further complicated by viewing the Bible as a source of truth about the academic disciplines, as was evident centuries ago concerning the interpretation of the psalm in light of Copernicus's discovery and as continues today in debates about the age of the earth.

The stakes of this battle got even higher in the second half of the twentieth century. In our effort to understand the tense relationship between the Bible and the academic disciplines, we note an important insight from a former headmaster and Christian-school leader, quoted as saying, "The Bible is not on trial in a Christian school."[26] The reference to the Bible on trial is significant; the twentieth century saw a battle rage in biblical scholarship between modernists, who challenged the Bible's inspiration, authority, inerrancy, and infallibility, and those who held firmly to a high view of Scripture. As this battle raged, the Supreme Court's decisions to remove prayer from public schools and the increased separation of church and state resulted in an explosion in evangelical Christian schooling. Research indicates Christian schools were being established at a pace of three per day.[27]

As this battle for the authority of the Bible raged and the number of Christian schools across America rapidly expanded, the centuries-old issue of how the Bible relates to the academic subjects remained a source of significant tension. Christian-school leaders no doubt felt great pressure to affirm the authority of the Bible as the infallible point of reference of our lives and the lives of our students. One statement by a leader in Christian schooling expresses well the battle lines at the root of the tension between the Bible and the academic subjects: "If some portion of a school textbook does not square with the Word of God, we simply say the textbook is in error on that point and that the Bible is correct. Our students must see us affirming the authority of the Scriptures."[28] The root of this tension is the expectation that God, who inspired the human authors of Scripture, intended it to be a source of truth about astronomy and the rest of the fields of academic study, prompting many to look to find in Scripture data or messages related to the study of the academic disciplines.[29]

WHAT INTEGRATION DOES NOT LOOK LIKE

Sometimes it is valuable to illustrate how best to view the relationship between the Bible and the academic disciplines by illustrating what not to do. A teacher is preparing a lesson to teach students how to practice good oral hygiene. Because he desires to include any input the Bible has about oral hygiene, he looks up "mouth" in a Bible concordance and finds a verse in Proverbs (21:23) that seems to fit very well: "Those who guard their mouths and their tongues keep themselves from calamity." The teacher decides to begin his lesson by quoting the verse.

This example illustrates a misunderstanding of the relationship between the Bible and the academic disciplines. Why would we expect the Bible to say anything about modern oral hygiene? By quoting the verse from Proverbs, the only thing added to student learning is the perpetuation of the distorted expectation that the Bible speaks to things such as oral hygiene and a corresponding message that truth discovered in the study of creation is a bit wobbly until it is strengthened by a scriptural reference. While nothing good is added to student learning by this view of Scripture, there is something lost. The main casualty is truth itself. In this example, the truth sacrificed is the actual meaning of the proverb about those who guard their mouths and tongues. In the case of Copernicus, the truth sacrificed was his discovery about the movement of the planets from the study of creation. The diagram below illustrates this misunderstood relationship:

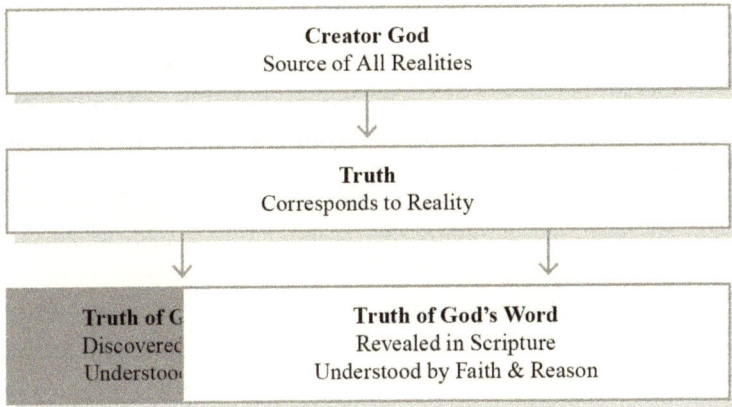

A Distorted View of the Truth of God's Word

In this view, the truth of God's Word extends into the truth of God's world, undermining students' ability to properly understand the way the two dimensions come together in a unity of all truth. The implications of this misunderstanding may reach further than one might think.

THE CONSEQUENCES OF A DISTORTED VIEW OF SCRIPTURE

Teaching students to view the Bible as a textbook that steamrolls or trumps the data from the field of science undermines their academic preparation. It also sends them out from our schools inadequately prepared to enter the academic arena of colleges and universities and armed with a distorted view of the Bible that handicaps, even prohibits, their ability to effectively engage the academic discipline from a perspective of a defensible Christian faith.[30] All too often this sets students from Christian schools up for a challenging confrontation when they are inundated, for example, with the data of science from the study of the natural world, presented to them by highly educated, respected, even winsome professors, in ways that are, or certainly appear to be, not only credible but compelling.

This confrontation is confusing and unsettling for students, and it exposes the inadequacy of the Bible-versus-science paradigm in which many were prepared. Some students go on the defense and fire back with arguments aimed at undermining the credibility of scientific data. Some of these arguments expose major theoretical assumptions that have been accepted without question in an academic discipline. Some of the arguments require intellectual contortions that shoehorn the data of science to accommodate previously determined interpretations of the message of the Bible, as in the case of Copernicus. In some unfortunate cases, Christian scientists spend less time engaging in open discussion and honest reflection to ensure that the science is in fact true—reflecting the way things really are in creation—and more time arguing dogmatically to make science fit a particular interpretation of Scripture. Some even resort to discrediting scientific ideas by discrediting the character of the people who make them, a practice that undermines the truth of the gospel far more than whatever idea may be proposed from science.

The most tragic consequence involves the students who in the face of opposing ideas experience a personal crisis and walk away from their faith, casualties of a misunderstanding of the relationship between the truth of the Bible and the truth of the natural world.[31] These casualties of faith can be avoided by teaching students to properly integrate Christian faith with the content of the academic disciplines. Day after day and year after year, students in Christian schools learn to read the truth of God's Word together with the truth of God's world, identifying the essential contribution each makes toward a unified and cohesive understanding of all truth. This is the heart of the Christian-school mission and is essential to helping students flourish.

A final consequence of Bible interpretations that steamroll rather than integrate the data of the academic disciplines is the undermining of Christian credibility in spiritual matters. This was a problem even in the fifth century, when Augustine noted that it was "a disgraceful and dangerous thing" for people who are not Christian, or perhaps even opposed to Christianity, to hear a Christian giving the supposed meaning from the Bible, while citing chapter and verse, yet talking nonsense about topics that many educated non-Christians know a great deal about from the study of the natural world. Augustine explained the real danger of this practice:

> If they find a Christian mistaken in a field which they themselves know well and hear him maintaining foolish opinions about our [Christian] books, how are they going to believe those books in matters concerning the resurrection of the dead, the hope of eternal life and the kingdom of heaven, when they think [the books'] pages are full of falsehoods on facts which they themselves have learnt from experience and the light of reason?[32]

Augustine's observation in the fifth century remains true in the twenty-first: an improper understanding of the relationship between the Bible and the academic disciplines marginalizes Christianity by engendering a perception that Christian thinking is untenable and anti-intellectual. Christians believe that general revelation and special revelation combine to form a complete perception of all created realities in the same way that both faith and reason work together to provide the most comprehensive and unified apprehension of truth that leads to human flourishing. To emphasize one in a way that restricts the other prohibits students' ability to fully engage culture with a clear and satisfying witness to the breadth of truth found in the full integration of faith with learning. Conversely, when faith and learning properly combine in a unified understanding of all truth, students become witnesses in the world of a complete and cohesive view of the world and life. This goal is at the heart of the distinctive mission of Christian schooling; genuinely integrating Christian faith with learning is the high calling and the high privilege of the Christian-school teacher.

Now we turn to some of the essential ideas that make this possible.

THE RELATIONSHIP BETWEEN THE BIBLE AND THE ACADEMIC DISCIPLINES

Having defined terms and outlined some unfortunate consequences of viewing the Bible as a textbook for the academic disciplines, we now look at the relationship between the Bible and the academic disciplines in a way that facilitates the integration of faith with learning. The first step is understanding the message of the Bible.

WHAT IS THE MESSAGE OF THE BIBLE?

The first step in this integration involves understanding the message of the Bible. For several reasons, Bible interpretation is not a simple matter. For starters, the timeline of the historical events recorded in the Bible spans not just centuries but millennia. Second, each book was written in a specific place and time reflecting a wide range of cultures, including ancient Near Eastern Palestine, Egypt, Persia during the Babylonian captivity, the region of Palestine during the time of Greece and Rome, and the New Testament letters written by Paul and others to churches throughout Asia Minor. Third, the Bible was originally written in different languages: the Old Testament in Ancient Hebrew with a few portions in Aramaic and the New Testament in Greek. Properly interpreting the text requires understanding the meaning of words in these languages at the time when the texts were written. Finally, the task of interpretation is complicated further because we do not have any of the original manuscripts. Biblical scholars must study small variations among the copies of extant ancient texts to determine which is likely closest to the original.

A whole field of knowledge called hermeneutics addresses the theory and method of interpreting the Bible and other ancient texts. The historical, cultural, and linguistic contexts as well as the textual data are studied to determine the text's meaning. Most seminaries teach hermeneutics to students preparing to preach and teach the Bible in many different contexts. Some Christian-school leaders believe teachers would benefit from a class in hermeneutics to better prepare them for the work of integrating Christian faith with learning.

Looking at the methods of Bible interpretation shows that the meaning of a Bible passage is not merely what the reader thinks, feels, or wants it to be. Rather, the foundational principle of hermeneutical theory is that the text means what the author intended it to mean when he wrote it. In the case of the Bible, there were many different human authors, each writing under the inspiration of the Holy Spirit, intending to communicate a specific message to specific people in a specific place. The high task of the biblical interpreter is first to determine the message that God, through the human author, intended to send in order to then apply its meaning to our current context. This is opposed to the common error known as "confirmation bias" where the interpreter simply looks to find data that is consistent with a bias or predetermined conclusion.

As we seek to understand the message of the Bible in the work of integration, historian Mark Noll suggests that an important first step is identifying what the Bible says about itself. He cites two passages that speak to the overall message of the Bible:

> But these [words of Scripture] are written that you may believe that Jesus is the Messiah, the Son of God, and that by believing you may have life in his name. (John 20:31)

> [F]rom infancy you have known the Holy Scriptures, which are able to make you wise for salvation through faith in Christ Jesus.

> All Scripture is God-breathed and is useful for teaching, rebuking, correcting and training in righteousness, so that the servant of God may be thoroughly equipped for every good work. (2 Timothy 3:15–17)

These passages clearly point to the message of the Bible as God's plan for salvation and spiritual truth. The confessions of the faith point in this same direction, affirming Scripture's testimony about itself as a revelation of God's plan of salvation in Jesus Christ. The Belgic Confession of 1561 first describes God's revelation of himself in nature and adds: "Second, God makes himself known to us more clearly by his holy and divine Word, as much as we need in this life, for God's glory and for our salvation."[33] Similarly, the Westminster Shorter Catechism answers question 3: "What do the Scriptures principally teach?" with the response, "The Scriptures principally teach, what man is to believe concerning God, and what duty God requires of man."[34]

Perhaps the most comprehensive contemporary description of the authority and high purpose of Scripture in the lives of believers is by renowned theologian J. I. Packer in his article "The Bible in Use: Evangelicals Seeking Truth from Holy Scripture." His description points us further in the same direction:

> Evangelicals maintain that as God has enthroned his Son, the living Word, as Lord of the universe, so he has enthroned the Bible, his written word, as the means of Christ's rule over the consciences of his disciples. The 66-book Protestant canon is held to be divinely inspired and authoritative, true and trustworthy, informative and imperative, life-imparting and strength-supplying to the human heart, and to be given to the church to be preached, taught, expounded, applied, absorbed, digested and appealed to as arbiter whenever questions of faith and life, belief and behavior, spiritual wisdom and spiritual welfare, break surface among the saints. Of the unifying bonds of evangelicalism, this view and use of Scripture is the strongest of all.[35]

God gave us the Bible to reveal, in a very direct and special way, who he is— his character and his desire for relationship seen through his intention for the world and human flourishing at the creation of all things, the distortion of the fall, and his immediate response to initiate a plan to restore creation, and his relationship to it, back to his original intention. This plan is now being accomplished as he, through his power, love, and wisdom, brings all things to completion at the end of time.

LIMITS OF SOURCES OF TRUTH

The foundation of the integration of faith in learning is understanding the *limits* or *boundaries*[36] that the teaching of Scripture places on the truth found in the created universe. For example, the study of creation presents compelling evidence for the existence of God, however, it cannot and does not fully reveal God's plan for the world and his desire to restore relationship with us made possible through the death of Christ on the cross. For this reason he gave us the Bible. Similarly, the Scriptures never claim that they are intended to "adjudicate directly all questions of human learning and human social organization."[37] For this we need the knowledge we gain from the study of the creation that is the focus of the academic disciplines. So rather than foes fighting to occupy the same territory, each reveals a separate and complementary dimension of truth that comes together, when properly interpreted, to form a cohesive and unified reflection of all truth—or the way things really are. Cornelius Plantinga expresses the complementary message this way: "Scripture tells us *who* created the wonders of the world, and *why*. Study of these wonders tells us, at least in part, *how* God did his wonders, and when. Both Scripture and science reveal God's nature and interests."[38]

A saying emerged in the wake of the Copernican revolution that captures the same idea: "The Bible shows the way to go to heaven, not the way the heavens go."[39] We have already highlighted the significant consequences that result when Christians expect the Bible to speak on matters about which it does not intend to speak. The converse is also true. Many scientists believe the data of science speak authoritatively about matters that extend beyond the limits of its data, including the existence of God, the ultimate origin of the universe, the meaning of life, and what happens when we die. In each case, the great casualty is a unified understanding of truth and reality that leads to human flourishing.

The truth discovered in the study of creation can never fully explain who God is, his desire for relationship with all he has made, the meaning of life, how we know right from wrong, what happens when we die—all this is revealed to us only in the Bible and understood by those who have faith. Similarly, the Bible does not reveal to us how the planets move in the universe, how cells divide to make new organisms, how to cure disease, how music works, the molecular structure of all things—all these truths have been discovered through the study of creation using the human capacity to reason.

Having defined the relationship between the truth of the Bible and the truth discovered in creation as essential partners with limits to understanding the truth of all created realities, we return to the example of the teacher preparing the lesson on oral hygiene for his elementary students. To accurately reflect this relationship, the teacher might introduce the lesson to elementary students this way:

> **Teacher:** "Students, who made the world and everything that is in it?"
>
> **Students:** "God made all that we see."
>
> **Teacher:** "And when God made people, what does the Bible say was special about people that he didn't say about other animals or plants or water and earth?"
>
> **Student:** "God made humans in his image."
>
> **Teacher:** "That's right. The fact that all people are made in the image of God gives them an ability to think, analyze, and study God's creation in ways that other parts of his creation cannot. In fact, you are using that ability right now in school, and someday you might use this ability to discover new things about the world God has made that might help us live healthier lives.
>
> "Today we are going to learn what scientists and dentists have discovered about how to have healthy teeth . . ."

This proper understanding of the relationship between the Bible and the academic disciplines opens the door to and facilitates the genuine integration of faith in learning. The cumulative process of integrated learning enables students to understand how the truth of Christian faith combines with their study of the academic subjects in a way that fits together to form a complete, unified explanation of the way things are in the world.

The power of an integrated education is its ability to satisfy the mind's most probing questions and the heart's deepest needs while casting a clear vision of what is required for students to flourish and become all they are capable of being.

DEFINING THE WAY FORWARD

Learning to read the truth of the Bible together with the truth of the natural world requires some humility on the part of scientists, because our knowledge of the truth of the natural world is incomplete. Meredith Kline, one of my seminary professors, was fond of saying, "The earth is as old as it is; the data is not all in yet." It also requires humility on the part of theologians, because our interpretation of the Bible may not be fully accurate. The best approach is to teach students to hold their beliefs unswervingly until the burden of proof requires a recalibration, as was the case with Copernicus. The Copernican revolution expanded our understanding of the natural world and our understanding of the Bible's message. Noll expresses a hopeful future direction in this critical area of reading the Bible together with the natural world:

> Satisfactory resolution of problems stemming from responsible biblical interpretation brought together with responsible interpretations of nature will not come easily. Such resolution requires more sophistication in scientific knowledge, more sophistication in biblical hermeneutics, and more humility of spirit than most of us possess. But it is not wishful thinking to believe that such resolution is possible.[40]

The students in Christian schools will be the beneficiaries of this clarified relationship for it will prepare them with a deeper understanding of the unity of truth.

CHAPTER SUMMARY

The idea of Christian schooling is defined by its mission to provide families with an educational option that brings together the truth discovered in the study of creation with the truth revealed in Scripture to form a cohesive and comprehensive understanding of the unity of all truth. Students come to understand it over time through daily instruction that integrates Christian faith with learning. Public schooling and all of culture reflect a marked disintegration of faith with learning due to a variety of factors including expanding pluralism and an increasingly strict separation of church and state. The calling and privilege of Christian-school teachers to integrate faith with learning requires a proper understanding of Scripture that resists seeking to view the Bible as speaking authoritatively about matters it does not intend to speak. An improper understanding of the relationship between the Bible and the academic disciplines undermines authentic integration and ultimately fails to prepare students to engage the world of ideas with a defensible faith. Rather than foes fighting to occupy the same territory, the truth of the Bible and the truth of academic disciplines are essential partners, each making a distinctive contribution toward understanding the truth of all created realities.

We turn now to the way integration is best accomplished—by means of the indispensable concept of worldview.

4

Introducing the Indispensable Concept of Worldview

"The concept of worldview constructs the arena in which the truth of God's special revelation in the Bible engages the truth of the God's general revelation in creation through the study of the academic disciplines."

—Tom Stoner

"Give me the child until he is seven, and I will give you the man."

—St. Ignatius of Loyola

After having attended a Christian high school, a Christian college, and seminary, and then after working as the head of a Christian school for fourteen years, I began work on my doctoral dissertation on teacher training for Christian schooling with a review of the literature on the philosophy of Christian schooling. When I turned to the literature on the concept of a Christian worldview, I was surprised at how essential a defined, intentional, and specific *worldview* was to the integration of Christian faith in classroom instruction. To that point I thought a Christian worldview was merely the way a person who is a Christian happens to look at the world. I realize that my experience may be unusual, but I have come to believe that the concept of *worldview* is the most widely used and poorly understood idea in Christian schooling today. It is also foundational to the Christian school mission and essential for human flourishing. As we explore this concept, consider how valuable it is to our students' effort to construct a complete picture of the world in which they live.

What exactly is a worldview? Though described using various terms, such as *grid, set of mental categories, frame of reference,* and *all-embracing life system,* each term refers to a particular way of looking at or thinking about the world.[41] We often use a lens for our eyes to help them view the world. A worldview is a lens through which the mind and heart see the world and all of life. This is only a starting place; a deeper understanding of this powerful concept will enable us to harness it as an indispensable tool for the integration of faith and learning.

James Sire, who has written extensively on worldview, defines it this way:

> A worldview is a commitment, a fundamental orientation of the heart, that can be expressed as a story or in a set of presuppositions (assumptions which may be true, partially true, or entirely false) that we hold (consciously or subconsciously, consistently or inconsistently) about the basic constitution of reality, and that provides the foundation on which we live and move and have our being.[42]

Just by reading the definition, we get a sense of its scope and importance, but few realize how pervasive a concept it is in each of our lives. In fact, David Naugle, another author who has written extensively on worldview, equates the concept with what it means to be human and describes it as an "inescapable" function of the human heart:

> [A worldview] creates the channels in which the waters of reason flow. It establishes the horizons of an interpreter's point of view by which texts of all types are understood. It is that mental medium by which the world is known. The human heart is its home, and it provides a home for the human heart.[43]

This is why the concept is so indispensable to our study on preparing students to flourish in their lives. We began by identifying that part of what it means to be human—made in the image of God—is to seek to understand and find answers to questions about the world. Worldview defines the questions all people everywhere seek to answer about the nature and meaning of life and also defines how their answers determine how they see the world and live their lives. No one has to assign humans the task of finding answers to these questions; rather, God has woven into the fabric of the human heart both the ability and the inclination to do so. Sire lists seven basic questions that constitute a worldview:

1. What is prime reality—the really real?

2. What is the nature of external reality, that is, the world around us?

3. What is a human being?

4. What happens to a person at death?

5. Why is it possible to know anything at all?

6. How do we know what is right from wrong?

7. What is the meaning of human history?[44]

There is a second important aspect of Sire's definition essential for our understanding of how students' worldviews are shaped. Worldviews are composed of a series of presuppositions—ideas that are assumed to be true without need for evidence or logical proof. This means a human constantly takes the stream of data he or she receives from daily life and human experience and intuitively places or assembles it, like the pieces of a puzzle, into the shape of a worldview or lens on the mind and heart. The data assembled into a worldview becomes central to the individual's identity and forms the basis from which he or she thinks, acts, and lives.

In our increasingly pluralistic society, the starting place from which people derive their understanding of these ultimate questions may differ radically. Sire catalogs the answers to these seven questions by the most commonly encountered worldviews of Christian Theism, Deism, Naturalism, Nihilism, Existentialism, Eastern Pantheistic Monism, The New Age—Spirituality Without Religion, Postmodernism, and Islamic Theism.[45] The shapes of individual worldviews, however, vary as widely as the people who hold them and may contain ideas from any or none of these common worldviews.

THE INFLUENCES THAT SHAPE A WORLDVIEW

It will be helpful to take a closer look at the almost unlimited sources that contribute to shaping a child's worldview from birth. The experiences and relationships of family and caregivers are almost certainly the most important, as are extended family, church, neighborhood, civic organizations, athletic teams, vocational choice and workplace, cultural traditions, and all human relationships and friendships. Then there are experiences related to physical health, mental and emotional health, wealth, poverty, marriage, divorce, race, warfare, sexual experiences, political associations, local, state, and national government, media, and social media. Among the most influential forces in a child's life we must also include the experiences and relationships in school. For all the reasons we have highlighted above, a child's schooling is worldview and life shaping.[46]

Each of these influences and many more constantly deposit data that collectively shape the human heart and construct a person's worldview. From this worldview every individual lives, acts, and makes decisions, some as simple as how to enjoy an hour of free time, others involving how to treat other people or choose a career. We live instinctively from our worldviews whether intentionally or intuitively, consciously or unconsciously: "Once the heart of an individual is formed by the powerful forces of both nature and nurture, it constitutes the presuppositional basis of life [which] constitutes the background logic for all thinking and doing."[47]

Far more than a privately held opinion about life that may or not be shared or engaged in the routines of daily life, worldviews have a specific utility: "A worldview is never merely a vision *of* life. It is always a vision *for* life as well."[48] All people think and act, knowingly or unknowingly, consistently or inconsistently, out of their individually constructed worldviews.

A child's earliest years of life and schooling are among the most powerful in shaping worldview. If you have ever watched a new house being built, you have likely observed that the most visible progress is made at the earliest stages when workers pour the foundation, frame the walls, and build the roof. Once the basic structure is in place, the progress toward completion is still very real but much less visible. Gaebelein noted the same dynamic when constructing a worldview: "The psychology of child development tells us that the early years are the most critical of all. It is then that character and emotional patterns are formed; it is then that the foundations of a Christian worldview are laid."[49] The Catholic Church and its vast network of schools has long been convinced of this truth as captured by the Jesuit maxim attributed to St. Ignatius of Loyola in the sixteenth century: "Give me the child until he is seven, and I will give you the man." In my work in Christian schooling, I speak with many parents who attended Catholic schools growing up and most are quick to acknowledge the influence of these years upon their current beliefs, convictions, and worldview.

WHY IS THE CULTIVATION OF A WORLDVIEW SO INFLUENTIAL IN A CHILD'S LIFE?

The belief systems in which children are raised—taught informally and formally in their homes, churches, and in their schools—are constantly giving children information about the way the world works and answering intuitive worldview questions, such as "How did we get here?" "What happens when we die?" "What is the meaning of life and history?" "What is wrong with things?" "How do we know what is right from wrong?" Sire uses the term *plausibility structure* to describe the belief system of a child's primary culture and its function of providing the child with a plausible view of the world and life.

Children benefit in some practical ways from receiving a clear and plausible view of the world and life when they are young. Elmer John Thiessen maintains that a stable and coherent primary culture that begins in the home and is supported by like-minded groups, organizations, or institutions is essential for children to cultivate a normal rationality and develop toward healthy autonomy: "It is rather obvious that children must be initiated into a particular home, a particular language, a particular culture, a particular set of beliefs before they can begin to expand their horizons beyond the present and the particular."[50] This is contrary to some who may believe the best, or perhaps even the only, way for children to learn to be autonomous, independent thinkers is to present them with a buffet of ideas and values from the start from which they can freely choose what to believe and how to live. Such a scenario is not only impossible, but also absurd. Children are born to parents, and they or designated caregivers are entrusted with the privilege and the high duty to care for and nurture them. This involves preparing them by modeling and through formal and informal instruction to understand right from wrong, good from bad, and what is worthy of honor or reproach, as part of a vision for what it means to flourish—a vision often rooted in the convictions of religious faith.

From this starting place of a coherent and consistent primary culture and attendant plausibility structure, children have a firm place to stand, a "ground zero,"[51] from which they can grow to become independent people who are able to think reflectively and critically. The path toward healthy autonomy requires a process of adolescence, during which children push back, forward, and sideways, kick the tires, and test the validity of the belief system in which they are raised. The best thing parents and caregivers can do to facilitate the path toward healthy autonomy is to provide a clear, complete, and cohesive belief system against which to push. Absent this, children are much more vulnerable to the powerful prevailing winds of popular culture. Many factors contribute to a coherent primary culture, but this path toward healthy autonomy is best accomplished in the context of a community with shared convictions.[52] Alongside the home, the church, and supporting organizations, the Christian school's intentional mission of worldview formation is a powerful addition to parents as they seek to pass on to their children their deeply held beliefs, values, and worldview.

DO CHRISTIAN SCHOOLS INDOCTRINATE?

Some would charge that the mission of Christian schools to provide students with a cohesive and comprehensive worldview that plausibly explains how the combined truth of God's world and Word create a unity of all truth is *indoctrination* rather than the healthiest path to prepare students to think for themselves. In a way, the charge is understandable; *indoctrination* simply defined means "causing to believe something," and the goal of instruction in Christian schools is to help students understand that which is true about the created realities of the world—including those revealed in the Bible that are understood by faith or belief. In this way, Christian schools absolutely want to cause students to believe something. But is this a hallmark of real and effective education, or is it indoctrination in a negative sense?

In chapter 1, we defined real education as never being neutral (an impossibility) but rather always resting upon an understanding of what is required for human beings to flourish, to be all they are capable of being; this involves making choices among competing visions. Private Christian schools exist to provide an option for parents that is real education, consistent with the family's understanding of what is required for human beings to flourish. We also considered the value of a school with a unified conception of human flourishing held in common by all school personnel and the majority of school families—an essential part of a stable primary culture that prepares children to think for themselves.

The value of a school designed this way is consistently supported in the research literature on effective schools. Moes and McCarty studied 123 private schools selected as "exemplary schools" by the US Department of Education and identified the top three factors shared by these effective schools: (1) close personal attention and genuine care of students by faculty and administration; (2) well-defined philosophies, perspectives, and values shared by parents and communicated to students; and (3) competent teachers motivated more by love for students and professional growth than by merit pay or status.[53] So a well-defined philosophy shared by all the stakeholders in a school community is a hallmark characteristic of an effective private school.

Other research studies confirm this. A 2011 study by the Canadian research-based Cardus Foundation analyzed a significant representative sample of Christian-school graduates aged twenty-four to thirty-nine. While controlling for more than thirty variables to isolate the impact of their schooling, the study found no evidence to support the stereotype that Christian schools are insular communities that breed divisive attitudes such as racism and moral criticism. To the contrary, the study found that the graduates of Protestant-Christian schools demonstrate a clear respect for authority and report a strong sense of direction in life, a confidence in their preparation for relationships, and a low incidence of feeling helpless in dealing with problems—all indications of being well-adjusted individuals ready to assume their places in society.[54] In light of the alignment of the mission of Christian schooling with the definition of real education and the support of research literature, a charge of indoctrination, even if based upon the simple definition of "causing to believe something," lacks sufficient warrant and sufficient understanding of effective teaching.

WHAT IS INDOCTRINATION?

But accusations remain, and in some cases justifiably. As commonly understood, the idea of indoctrination sounds imposing for it is associated with coercive methods that look more like brainwashing, programming, and disseminating propaganda than typical classroom instruction. But there is an important theme marking any type of indoctrination that involves a governing authority that filters information in keeping with a predetermined bias and limits free inquiry and open intellectual exploration.

We witnessed a clear example of indoctrination with a middle-school student who came to America from a country ruled by an authoritarian government known for restricting the information made available to the citizenry. The middle-school student was asked to write a paper on someone she considered a hero. Not surprisingly, she chose her country's authoritarian leader and cited several reasons she had been told from the time she was very young. Now, however, she had access to information that was not limited to one particular perspective or tightly controlled by a governing authority. The teacher encouraged her to learn more about her country and its leadership from multiple new sources. After this exercise in free inquiry and open intellectual exploration, the student realized the extent of her limited understanding; there was additional information to which she had not been exposed. She responded by choosing an alternate hero, this time a teenage pop star! This example clearly meets both criteria for indoctrination: a governing authority filtering content according to a predetermined bias and a limit to free inquiry and open exploration. Let's consider another example.

The story is told of a Christian high school that employed a biology teacher whom students liked very much. She did what good teachers do: presented the academic content in creative ways that made it easier to understand. One day, in the middle of the year, she disappeared. According to the student grapevine, a student in one of her classes had discovered and reported to his father—a school board member—that the teacher held beliefs about evolution that were for some reasons unacceptable. Her students were disappointed that she had left and wondered just what those reasons were, yet they never learned the ideas she believed and why they were a problem. Where and when else were they supposed to explore these ideas if not in their high school biology class? Were the students better off for not having been exposed to her beliefs?

Some Christian schools confuse the mission of Christian schooling—to teach students the academic content in every subject integrated with the truth of Christian faith through the lens of a Christian worldview—with teaching students *only* the academic content that is consistent with Christian faith and values. There is a big difference. The former is consistent with the definition of real education, provides students with a cohesive view of all truth, and prepares students well for academic pursuits after high school.

The latter is more consistent with the definition of indoctrination—limiting or filtering the academic content to what agrees with Christian faith or, perhaps more accurately, to what agrees with a particular interpretation of the Bible. The motivation is no doubt sincere and born of a desire to align children's beliefs with the authoritative teaching of Scripture. The important question, however, is this: when will the students in the Christian school learn, or be taught, to understand the landscape of ideas and perspectives in the content of the academic disciplines and evaluate those ideas and perspectives from a Christian worldview?

In any school setting, an administrator or teacher does not need to believe something to be the most viable viewpoint—or even viable at all—to find ample justification to present it to students. In fact, students learn to know why they believe something to be true and why they believe something to be false by freely exploring all ideas and considering the data that supports a given perspective, the data that conflicts with a given perspective, and the data that is merely assumed, or presupposed, to be true. For Christian schools to build a strong academic foundation, they must teach all the academic content necessary for the students to be prepared not only for the next grade level or to meet the school's graduation requirements, but ultimately to be prepared for academic study in whatever college they choose. At the same time, for Christian schools to fulfill their distinctive mission to integrate Christian faith in learning, they must teach the full breadth of the academic content at each grade level through the powerful concept of a Christian worldview.

THE SPECTRUM OF INDOCTRINATION

Do Christian schools indoctrinate? The answer is a decisive no if the charge is leveled by someone who believes that teaching the full landscape of ideas in each academic discipline from a unified worldview is itself indoctrination. This is what defines the distinctive mission of Christian schools; it is why they exist and what Christian parents deeply value about them. Their ability to provide students with a cohesive and comprehensive worldview that plausibly explains how the truth of God's world and God's Word combine to create a unity of all truth is key to their life-shaping power. Free and unrestricted intellectual inquiry from a unified worldview is not indoctrination.

Public schools and nonreligious private schools provide a variety of worldviews from textbooks, multiple teachers, and school policies from which students interpret meaning and understanding of the world. While some of the messages they receive conflict with others, the thread woven throughout is the pervasive worldview of contemporary society, best summarized as a unified philosophy of secularism—possibly itself indoctrination. We have also identified the increasingly strict separation of church and state in public schools as a contributing factor to the pervasive disintegration of Christian faith with learning in society today. This public policy requirement restricting the presentation of Christian ideas and content also meets the definition of indoctrination. The most practical way to view the question of whether a school indoctrinates is not answered by a simple yes or no, but by using a spectrum.

$\longleftarrow \hspace{6cm} \longrightarrow$

Limited Inquiry   Free & Open Inquiry
According to Bias   Full Landscape of Ideas

The Spectrum of Indoctrination

All schools fall somewhere on the spectrum. Public schools filter the content of religious faith. Many private schools filter traditional perspectives on marriage, sexuality, and gender. Other schools and academic departments filter according to a certain political ideology. Some Christian schools teach only ideas that are consistent with faith and values, while others encourage a thorough exploration of the full landscape of ideas on a given topic, relying on the teacher to integrate faith with learning by bringing a Christian worldview to bear on all content.

Why is any of this important? The whole purpose of this book is to help parents and grandparents select a school that will contribute to the flourishing of the child they love while knowing what to expect from the school of their choice. Christian schools must identify where they currently fall on the spectrum and determine if where they are is where they intend to be. Board members at the schools might receive a presentation and discuss these important matters, so they know where their school stands and are prepared to communicate to all stakeholders. Parents, both current and prospective, want to know what to expect from their Christian school. One parental question I frequently answer is, how do you teach science?

In nearly every case, it is important for the parent to hear that we want our students to understand all ideas, including (especially?) the theory of evolution and how to engage it from a Christian worldview. Finally, teachers need to understand where a school falls on the spectrum, to understand the expectations for how they will teach and determine if a school is a good fit for a long tenure.

THE OUTWARD FOCUS OF A CHRISTIAN WORLDVIEW

One of the most valuable characteristics of the worldview concept is its transferability: the ease by which it can be overlaid, like a grid on a transparency, on any idea, historic event, story, movie, conversation, book, or cultural phenomenon. The concept of worldview by its very definition is outward looking. It facilitates engagement between the Christian and culture as well as deepens the level at which cultural engagement occurs. The outward focus of a worldview differs from the study of biblical doctrine known as *systematic theology*.

HOW IS A WORLDVIEW DIFFERENT FROM SYSTEMATIC THEOLOGY?

Over the course of history, Christian thinkers and Bible scholars have developed systematic theology as an organized way of interpreting the content of the Bible using the major doctrinal categories of Bibliology (the study of the Bible), Theology Proper (the study of God), Christology (the study of Christ), Pneumatology (the study of the Holy Spirit), Anthropology (the study of humanity), Soteriology (the study of Salvation), Ecclesiology (the study of the church), Eschatology (the study of the end times), and Angelology (the study of angelic beings). Art Holmes highlights this important distinction between systematic theology and worldview: "A systematic theology looks in at revelation; a worldview looks out at creation."[55] The value and function of a systematic theology is as a tool of Bible study and interpretation that helps facilitate one's understanding of the Christian faith. The various doctrines are like individual trees that combine to form the content of the Christian faith. A worldview is different. A worldview is like a forest that is shaped by the content of Scripture, including the study of theology, and it looks outward at the world. To change the illustration, the study of systematic theology generates the individual books that together form the content of the Christian faith; the concept of worldview is the shelves on which the individual books rest.[56]

With a view of the forest rather than individual trees, the concept of worldview transcends the theological differences among various Christian groups. One never hears of "the Baptist worldview," because the concept of worldview operates at the level of the forest not the trees. Systematic theologies vary according to interpretive communities. In fact, the existence of the different interpretative communities—Catholic and Protestant, the various orders in Catholicism and denominations within Protestantism—are defined by variations in the interpretation and practice of the teachings of the Christian faith. Such differences have emerged throughout history as each interpretive community looked inward at God's revelation in the Bible, and these differences are reflected in one of the areas of systematic theology. For example, Catholics and Protestants differ significantly on the doctrine of the church and the way it is structured and governed, the doctrine of the Bible and how it is viewed in relation to other church teaching, and the doctrine of salvation or the means by which a person is saved.

Within Protestantism, the Reformed traditions, following the teaching of John Calvin, emphasize the sovereign work of God in bringing people to salvation, while non-Reformed traditions emphasize human responsibility in salvation, following the teaching of James Arminius and John Wesley. Lutherans follow the teachings of Martin Luther; Baptists emphasize their view on baptism, and Congregationalists the role of the congregation in governing the church.

As a valuable part of the academic program, Christian schools provide students with formal instruction in Bible and theology. If an individual school aligns with a particular interpretative community, families whose faith tradition is different from the faith tradition of the school must anticipate some robust theological discussions around the dinner table when students share their notes from class lectures and the ideas they are learning in Bible class. Such learning is what education is all about and is valuable both for the student and the family.

However, when it comes to the defining characteristic of Christian schooling to teach literature, math, science, and all of the academic subjects from a Christian worldview, a worldview's outward focus at creation and culture combined with its "forest view" of the overarching themes of

Scripture (creation, fall, redemption, consummation) make it possible for students from a wide variety of interpretive communities to flourish in a particular school community. The same qualities of a worldview also make it possible for schools from a variety of Christian traditions to collaborate toward making schools more effective and distinctive.

WHY IS WORLDVIEW CENTRAL TO CHRISTIAN SCHOOLING?

Among the most valuable contributions the concept of worldview provides students is the way it constructs the arena in which the truth of God's special revelation in the Bible engages the truth of God's general revelation in creation through the study of the academic disciplines. This facilitates and enlivens the ability of Christians to engage culture and the academic disciplines with a defensible faith and provides touch points by which students are able to grab hold, engage, analyze, and dialogue with ideas that may vary widely from their own. The value of worldview analysis in the academic setting is central to the distinctive nature of Christian schooling.

In the school context, the point of contact between the Christian faith and the academic content is not often a particular Bible passage or biblical doctrine. Rather, academic study is processed, with many points of contact, through a broader grid, framework, or lens on the mind and heart—the Christian worldview.

AN EXAMPLE OF WORLDVIEW FACILITATING ACADEMIC AND CULTURAL ENGAGEMENT

Let me illustrate. I surveyed a group of current teachers who were identified by their administrators as having ten or more years of experience in a Christian school and were viewed by their colleagues, students, and parents as being effective teachers in their particular academic disciplines *and* as Christian-school teachers. I asked the teachers this question: In what ways is the academic content of the class/classes you teach different at your Christian school than it would be if you taught the same class/classes at a public school?

Two starkly contrasting answers illustrate the limited ways the Bible directly relates to the academic content and the vigorous cultural and academic engagement facilitated by the concept of worldview.

> Teacher 1: There is very little difference. We are encouraged to integrate faith and our subject areas. I have had students memorize Bible verses—Psalm 19:1–4 and Colossians. I usually start class by reading a Bible passage. I do this because I am a scientist and a Christian and I want to show my students that both of these things are important to me. [High School Science: Chemistry 10, Physics]

> Teacher 2: If our culture were one where the approach to science was based on the classical definition of science, such as that concisely furnished by Webster that "Science is defined as a systematized knowledge derived from observation, study, and experimentation carried on in order to determine the nature or principles of what is being studied" (1983), the academic content would be exactly the same. However, science is not presented with this limitation but rather includes philosophical and religious components based on atheistic naturalism [a worldview]. Therefore, our approach to instruction must vary. The position of our school in general and our science department in particular is that objective science should be approached without any a priori limitations and the data gained by experimentation be allowed to lead to the most robust and sensible scientific conclusions. This inclusive position allows for the possibility of supernatural intervention into the creation and operation of the physical universe. Allowing this possibility requires that the definition of science based only on naturalism be specifically rejected, a major difference from instruction in the public sector and, sadly, in some Christian institutions.
>
> From a position resting on a robust scientific foundation favoring theism, the approach to the sciences at our school allows the viewpoint that all physical systems are the result of the actions of a supernatural transcendent Creator. This viewpoint holds that all matter and the laws that govern its behavior were created in the past and have teleological significance and a purpose. This is a stark contrast to the position of the naturalist, which cannot posit any teleological inference whatsoever due to the constraints of the a priori assumptions of naturalism and the view of science resulting from that assumption. The texts we use, and those that are used exclusively in the public sector, are based on philosophical conjectures that do impose a priori constraints on the study of science. These texts (physics texts not so much but life science

texts are saturated with these conjectures) invariably begin with an atheistic bias and proceed on the assumption that science can only be approached naturalistically. The authors then adroitly interweave that which has been established by scientific means with past and current conjectures of how things originated and how they change, all under the umbrella of the dogma of neo-Darwinism or some other allied worldview.

The Christian worldview, on the other hand, makes scientific claims about the very same subjects as the naturalist, claiming that the whole of creation is the direct result of the actions of a supernatural Creator, a position diametrically opposed to the assertions of those holding the naturalist worldview.

The core of this conflict is simply and concisely stated by the evolutionist Futuyma, who . . . is profoundly correct. He writes: "Creation and evolution, between them, exhaust the possible explanations for the origin of living things. Organisms either appeared on the earth fully developed or they did not. If they did not, they must have developed from preexisting species by some process of modification. If they did appear in a fully developed state, they must indeed have been created by some omnipotent intelligence, for no natural process could possibly form inanimate molecules into an elephant or redwood tree in one step . . ." (Douglas Futuyma, *Science on Trial: The Case for Evolution*, 197). These two worldviews cannot be reconciled so of necessity instructional time is devoted to building a step-by-step comparison of the two positions. The stated purpose of the science program at our school is to equip students to think critically and objectively about any scientific evidence presented. As part of the curriculum in the sciences and in other courses, students study the claims of both the naturalistic and theistic worldviews and develop an understanding of the philosophical and ethical ramifications of each. This is generally not possible in the public sector as any worldview other than atheistic naturalism is not tolerated, which is sad as it limits the students' ability to think critically.[57]

The more lengthy response is a good example of the specific skill of biblical worldview integration in science and the distinctive model of classroom instruction Christian schools at their best provide students. Students benefit from this type of instruction as the concept of worldview facilitates authentic integration by constructing the arena in which the truth of the Christian faith engages with and explores the truth found in creation in the study of the academic disciplines. The result is a deep and unified understanding of truth.

```
┌─────────────────────────────────────────────┐
│                Creator God                   │
│            Source of All Realities           │
└─────────────────────────────────────────────┘
                      ↓
┌─────────────────────────────────────────────┐
│                   Truth                      │
│            Corresponds to Reality            │
└─────────────────────────────────────────────┘
            ↓                    ↓
┌───────────────────────┬───────────────────────┐
│  Truth of God's World │  Truth of God's Word  │
│         Reason        │     Faith & Reason    │
└───────────────────────┴───────────────────────┘

                Education and
                Culture Today
      ↓                              ↓
┌──────────────┐                ┌──────────────┐
│   Academic   │  ← Disintegration → │  Christian   │
│  Disciplines │                │     Faith    │
└──────────────┘                └──────────────┘

        ┌───────────────────────────────┐
        │       Biblical Worldview      │ ←
        └───────────────────────────────┘
              ↓        ↓        ↓
        ┌───────────────────────────────┐
      → │      Academic Disciplines     │
        └───────────────────────────────┘
                      ↓
┌─────────────────────────────────────────────┐
│               Unity of Truth                 │
└─────────────────────────────────────────────┘
                      ↓
┌─────────────────────────────────────────────┐
│        Academic & Cultural Engagement        │
└─────────────────────────────────────────────┘
```

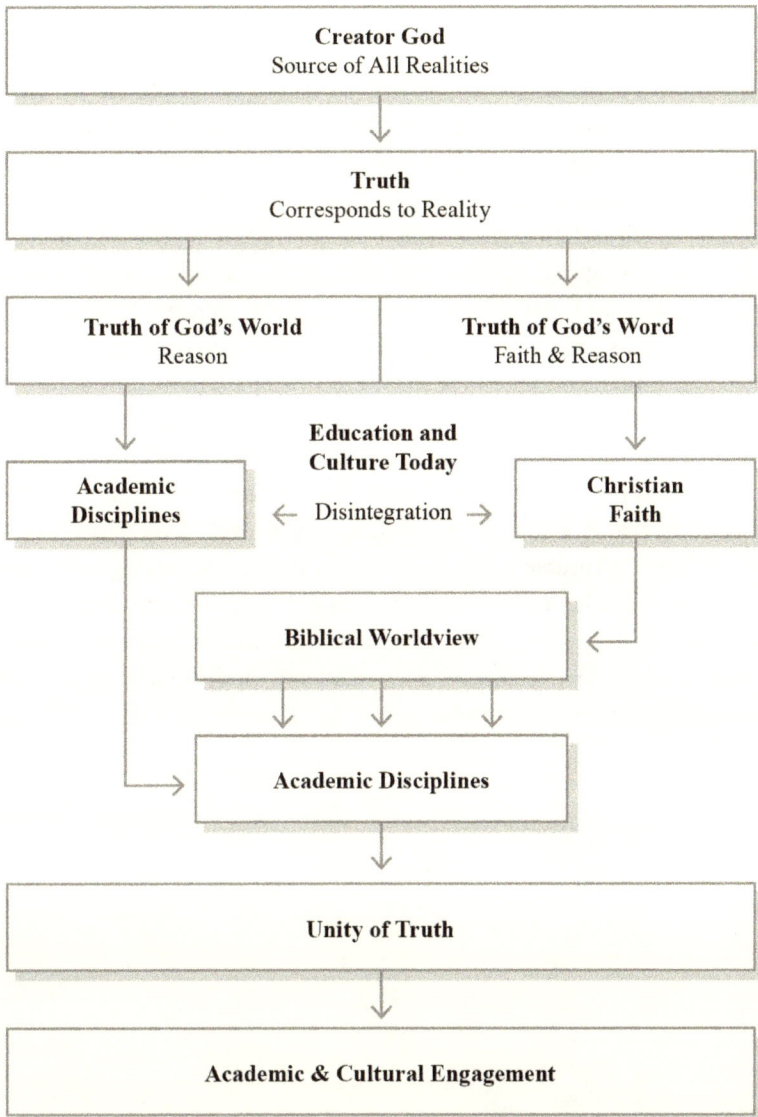

Worldview Facilitates Academic and Cultural Engagement

The concept of worldview is indispensable to the idea of a Christian school and undergirds the threefold mission of Christian schooling to which we now turn our attention.

CHAPTER SUMMARY

Worldview is a widely used and poorly understood concept indispensable to the idea of a Christian school. It is an inescapable function of what it means to be human and created in the image of God and is a lens on the mind and heart formed as all people seek to answer ultimate questions about the meaning of life. Worldview is central to a person's identity and becomes the foundation from which life is lived. A myriad of influences contribute to shaping individual worldviews, including family, religion, schooling, and all types of relationships and experiences. The early years are critical to its formation and a stable worldview provides students with a plausible understanding of life that becomes a path to healthy autonomy. The shared values by all stakeholders in a Christian school are a hallmark of an effective private school and is different from indoctrination as it encourages free and open inquiry into all ideas. Worldview differs from systematic theology in that it looks out at creation at the level of the forest not the trees. It is indispensable to the mission of Christian schooling as it creates the arena in which Christian faith is brought together with the academic disciplines in a unity of truth. Specialized classroom instruction from a Christian worldview facilitates deep academic and cultural engagement that contribute to human flourishing.

5

Academic Formation

Essential Preparation for a Child's Future

"Just as restaurants had better have good food, our Christian schools had better offer a program that builds a strong academic foundation for students—if the schools hope to thrive in the future as the costs of education continue to rise."

—Tom Stoner

"[God] wants a child's heart, but a grown-up's head . . . God is no fonder of intellectual slackers than of any other slackers."

—C. S. Lewis

Instruction in All Academic Subjects	Instruction from a Christian Worldview	Nurturing Christian Faith & Character
↓	↓	↓
Academic Formation	Christian Worldview Formation	Spiritual Formation

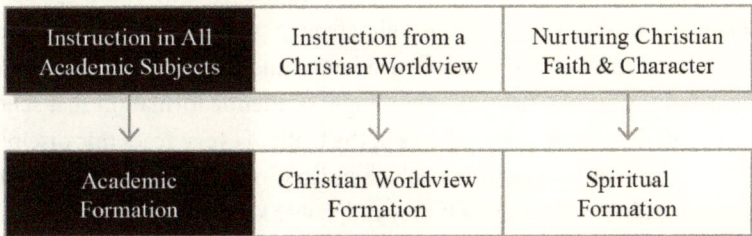

The Christian-School Mission of Academic Formation

In my conversations with all stakeholders within Christian schooling—parents, faculty, prospective parents, grandparents, donors, as well as colleagues working in public and private schools that are not faith based, the idea to which I most frequently refer is the focus of this chapter and the two following: the threefold mission of Christian schooling. The threefold mission of Christian schooling captures the idea of a Christian school, identifies its life-shaping impact upon students, and illustrates why it offers such a distinctive option in the private-school marketplace. The threefold mission of Christian schooling explains (1) academic formation, the aspect of our mission that is similar or even identical to public and nonreligious private schools; (2) Christian worldview formation, the aspect of our mission that is completely distinctive to Christian schooling; and (3) spiritual formation, the aspect of the Christian-school mission that is similar or even identical with that of a church youth group or the outstanding parachurch ministries such as Young Life, the Fellowship of Christian Athletes, and the like. All three aspects of the Christian-school mission are essential to human flourishing and helping children become all they are created to be.

INTRODUCTION TO THE ACADEMIC MISSION

I remember walking a prospective parent around the school in Boston where I was head. As I described our distinctly Christian program, I could tell by his affirming nods, attentiveness, and pleasant comments that he liked what he saw and was positively disposed. When we finished the tour, I asked if he had any questions. He hesitated before saying, "I just want to make sure of something: now you teach math, science, history, and stuff like that here, right?" I assured him that we certainly did. I guess he just wanted to be extra sure we were more than a church youth group that met all day every day and charged tuition!

What separates a Christian school from a church youth group—or what distinguishes Christian schooling from a program of Christian education in churches—is the school's academic mission. A school is a school, and a major goal of Christian schooling is academic formation that schools accomplish by instructing students in the truth of every academic discipline. Church youth groups do not teach chemistry, math, writing, and the other academic subjects. I imagine if they did, fewer kids would choose to attend!

This basic model of teaching children the core content and skills in every academic discipline has been adopted around the world and proven over millennia to be effective in educating children to understand the world as part of becoming productive members of society. This certainly includes the United States, where every child is offered free access to public education, regulated state by state. The federal government sets policies and prescribes national standards for the content and skills that each state must teach students at each chronological grade level. It also creates nationwide tests to assess each state's progress toward meeting the standards, all in an effort to ensure that students are equipped with the essential knowledge and skills for the next level of study, to meet graduation requirements, to enter college if desired, and ultimately to live and work in society. All schools—Christian, public, and all other private schools—share the same academic mission to prepare students to meet or exceed the academic standards established by the state and federal governments. This also means that the training teachers receive in state universities and private secular colleges transfers directly to the academic mission of Christian schools.

Christian schools enter the private-school marketplace to offer families an alternative option for their children's education that is consistent with their vision for human flourishing rooted in Christian faith by integrating that faith with the study of the academic disciplines. The integration of Christian faith into learning does not alter the fact that the mission of Christian schools is to educate—to instruct children in the content of the academic subjects at every grade level. In fact, research studies confirm that parents choose private schools both for an education consistent with their religious beliefs and for a quality of academic instruction that exceeds that which is offered in the tuition-free public schools. In other words, parents want a Christian school to be a place of academic formation *and* spiritual formation. Unfortunately, there is often a tense perception that they are mutually exclusive, so you must pick one or the other. Why is this perception so common?

TENSION BETWEEN ACADEMIC LEARNING AND CHRISTIAN FAITH

Tertullian, one of the early church fathers, famously asked the question, "What does Athens have to do with Jerusalem?" Athens was the location of Plato's Academy of Athens, the first school of higher education in the Western world, making Athens a symbol for the triumph of human reason to understand the truth found in the study of created realities. Jerusalem was the epicenter of Jesus's life, death, and resurrection, making Jerusalem a symbol of the Christian faith and the ministry of the church. Tertullian's question in the second century AD reveals how the relationship between reason and faith, the university and the church, and the study of God's world and his Word, has been marked more by strife than peace. I propose three contributing factors.

FAITH VERSUS REASON?

The perception of Christian faith as being irrational and something for the simple-minded is nothing new. Faith is faith, and because faith precedes a complete and rational understanding of all the created realities, those who do not have Christian faith are prone to scoff at the perceived "blind leap" of logic required to be a Christian. The second-century Greek philosopher Celsus exemplifies such a scoffer as he identified who may enter the Christian community: "Let no educated man enter, no wise man, no prudent man, for such things we deem evil; but whoever is ignorant, whoever is unintelligent, whoever is uneducated, whoever is simple, let him come and be welcome."[58]

This tension has been exacerbated in the wake of the Enlightenment, which elevated reason to the sole standard of truth, deeming any idea that relies on faith as myth or superstition. On the other side of the spectrum, some Christians equate the appreciation of reason and academic pursuits with being "worldly." Others see reason as dangerous and a threat to one's spiritual mission; to bolster their view, they might mention the well-documented departure of our nation's oldest colleges from their original mission, to prepare pastors for Christian ministry.

POOR BIBLE INTERPRETATION

Some Christians interpret the apostle Paul's statement in 1 Corinthians that "knowledge puffs up while love builds up," in a way that discounts the value of education in general and highlights its danger. To be sure, intellectual pride is a real danger, but the phrase in the context of Paul's argument reads: "Now about food sacrificed to idols: We know that 'We all possess knowledge.' But knowledge puffs up while love builds up. Those who think they know something do not yet know as they ought to know. But whoever loves God is known by God" (1 Corinthians 8:1–3).

Paul is addressing a controversy in the church in Corinth about eating food that has been sacrificed to idols. Understanding the context of a passage is essential if one is to accurately interpret its meaning and apply it to today. It distorts the meaning of the Bible text to simply lift the words "knowledge puffs up while love builds up" from the teaching about food sacrificed to idols and apply it to mean something about the value of education in the twenty-first century. Consider another example. Some interpret Jesus's words in Matthew 18:3, "Truly I tell you, unless you change and become like little children, you will never enter the kingdom of heaven," to mean that education undermines faith. But here Jesus uses the way a child accepts what she hears as true without needing to be convinced to illustrate that faith precedes understanding about the truth of God's Word. One enters the kingdom of heaven by accepting God's Word like a child, and one's faith grows by accepting God's truth from the same childlike posture. Yet faith combined with our God-given capacity to reason enables us to grasp a complete and cohesive understanding of all truth. In *Mere Christianity*, C. S. Lewis quips about this text that God "wants a child's heart, but a grown-up's head . . . God is no fonder of intellectual slackers than of any other slackers."[59]

HEART PREVAILING OVER MIND

Occasionally some Christian leaders contribute to the suspicion of education like the well-documented nineteenth-century revivalists who seemed to turn their backs on academia or intellectualism as they heralded the need for personal conversion. Or there's the Christian school leader who said, "The main focus in Christian school education today should be on character, not occupation; on living rather than learning."[60] Such statements are undoubtedly intended to emphasize the Christian-school mission of spiritual formation. I would be more critical of such statements or include other foolish sounding quotes from Christian leaders, but to be honest, I remember, nearly twenty years ago in my early years as a Christian-school head, telling a faculty member, "The particular academic subject doesn't really matter, it is only a tool to gain access to a student's heart." I was leading a Christian school at the time! I, too, was emphasizing the priority of our spiritual mission, but why did I feel the need to throw the academic subject matter under the bus? The academic subjects do matter especially as we build our students' academic foundations in the context of private Christian schooling.

BREAKING THE TENSION

Whether a result of an improper understanding of the relationship of faith to reason or poor Bible interpretation or a simple desire to prioritize the Christian-school mission of spiritual formation, there is a long-standing tension between academic learning and Christian nurture that views them to be mutually exclusive: you can have one or the other but not both. I remember a parent saying, "You seem to be talking a lot about academics; people fear that you are de-emphasizing our Christian mission." This articulates an unacceptable paradigm, with academic formation and spiritual formation on a single-line spectrum as pictured below.

←——————————————————————————————→

Christian Faith   Academics
and Character

The Common Misconception of Faith and Learning

In the mind of so many, the further one moves toward one end, the further one moves away from the other. Many people—parents and caregivers, even Christian-school teachers and administrators (like me years ago!)—see this spectrum as the only option and search for the ideal place on the spectrum. Would that be in the middle? A little favored toward spiritual nurture? Or perhaps because of the support of the local church and parachurch ministries, a little favored toward academics?

There is not, however, one spectrum, but two, as pictured below.

Academic Formation

←——————————————————————————————→

Poor Quality   High Quality

Spiritual Formation

←——————————————————————————————→

Ineffective   Highly Effective

The Proper Understanding of the Mission of Christian Schooling

The mission of Christian schooling is to prepare our students for their futures by being toward the high-quality end of both.

AFFIRMING THE ACADEMIC MISSION

Study after study shows that parents are drawn to Christian schools for their Christian mission and vision of human flourishing consistent with their deeply held convictions of Christian faith. These same parents rightly expect a school to be a school. Just as restaurants had better have good food, our Christian schools had better offer a program that builds a strong academic foundation for students—if the schools hope to thrive in the future as the costs of education continue to rise. Christian schools, like all schools, have an academic mission! As we introduce our schools to all our stakeholders—current and prospective parents, grandparents, and people in the local community—what is wrong with simply saying, "We are a Christian school. We study history, math, English, science, foreign language and so on, and we study them very well indeed"?[61]

We want our teachers constantly telling their students, "We are here today for you to use the minds God has given you to understand the truth discovered through the study of the world God has made brought together with the truth revealed in the study of God's Word so you can assemble a complete picture of the world in which we live. We do this through the study of math, science, art, literature, Bible, music, etc., so that you are academically prepared for tomorrow, next school year, graduation, college, and ultimately to find your passion, vocation, and calling for the future." The threefold mission of Christian schooling to prepare students for that place begins with academic formation, through the finest instruction in all the academic disciplines.

We turn now to the second aspect of the threefold mission of Christian schooling: cultivating students' Christian worldview.

CHAPTER SUMMARY

The mission of academic formation in Christian schools is identical to public schools and other private schools. The model of teaching students the core content and skills of all the academic disciplines has been embraced for millennia around the world as essential preparation for children to flourish in society. There is a long-standing perception that academic learning and

Christian faith are mutually exclusive rooted in the complex relationship between faith and reason, poor Bible interpretation, and Christian leaders' desire to prioritize spiritual formation. Parents of students in Christian schools want a high-quality academic education to prepare their children for the next school year, graduation, college, and a future vocational calling.

6

Christian Worldview Formation

How It Happens and the Difference It Makes

"The best preparation for encountering false ideas is to know what is true."

—TOM STONER

"The Christian faith is a very definite thing, with sharp doctrinal edges. It has a certain shape. That is why it is called the Faith. Unless your worldview conforms to that shape, it is not a Christian worldview."

—RICHARD RIESEN

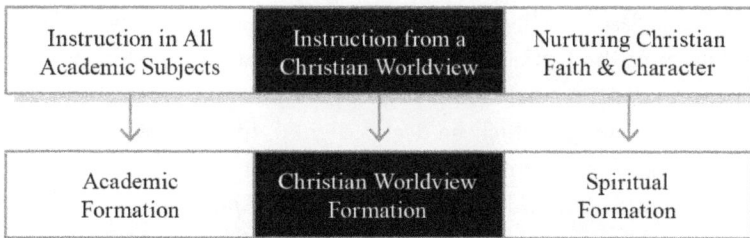

Instruction in All Academic Subjects	Instruction from a Christian Worldview	Nurturing Christian Faith & Character
↓	↓	↓
Academic Formation	Christian Worldview Formation	Spiritual Formation

The Mission of Christian Worldview Formation

If academic formation is the area in which the Christian-school mission is identical to that of public schools and private schools that are not intentionally Christian, then this second area—Christian worldview formation—is entirely distinctive to the Christian school. Building upon the introduction to worldview in chapter 4, in this chapter we look at how our students' worldviews are formed—or how the lenses of their hearts are minds are shaped to view the world and life consistent with the truth of Christian faith. This will require us to define the shape of a Christian worldview, identify how it is formed, look more closely at the contribution of instruction in the Christian-school classroom, and clarify why worldview formation is so valuable in preparing students to flourish in college and in life.

WHAT DOES A CHRISTIAN WORLDVIEW LOOK LIKE?

A Christian worldview is particular, specific, and objective, because Christian faith is particular, specific, and objective. A person with a Christian worldview answers ultimate questions about the meaning of life and how we know right from wrong differently than a person whose worldview is shaped by Buddhism, new age spirituality, or atheistic naturalism. This is Reisen's point:

> A Christian worldview is not simply what you or I happen to think or feel. A worldview is itself an academic thing, requiring [it] to be informed, disciplined, thought through . . . The Christian faith is a very definite thing, with sharp doctrinal edges. It has a certain shape. That is why it is called The Faith. Unless your worldview conforms to that shape, it is not a Christian worldview.[62]

But what shape is it? The shape of a Christian worldview is the shape of God's revelation of himself, his truth, and his plan for the world in Scripture. Naugle describes the process of constructing a worldview as "clothing the content of the Christian faith in the garment of a worldview."[63] That garment retains the overarching shape of Scripture: God's intention at the *creation* of all things, which he declared good, the disruption of the created order resulting from the *fall* of humankind in the garden of Eden, the immediate initiation and gracious plan of *redemption* in the person and work of Jesus Christ to restore the creation to his original intention, and the anticipated completion or *consummation* of the work of restoration at the end of time in the new heavens and earth. Creation, Fall, Redemption, and Consummation are the overarching themes of Scripture and the pillars giving shape to the garment of a Christian worldview.

WORLDVIEW FORMATION AND LEARNING MORE OF JESUS CHRIST

Christian worldview formation requires a deep and thorough understanding of the truth of Scripture through intentional, disciplined study over time. While there may have been a day when the family and the church provided substantial theological education to children, the practice is increasingly rare. How then will students and all school personnel gain an understanding of Scripture broad enough to encompass the whole of God's revelation and deep enough to cultivate a healthy Christian worldview?

The addition of instruction in Bible to the standard curriculum in Christian schools is very helpful to deepen students' understanding. The Confessions used by some theological traditions are also valuable tools to deepen students' knowledge of Scripture. Historian Mark Noll sees the historic Christian creeds as indispensable tools to ground Christian faith because of the way they distill or boil down biblical truth to the essentials of the faith—each phrase having been discussed, debated, and carefully selected by theologians to combat error and provide Christians with time-tested truth.

> The ancient creeds became authoritative in the early centuries because they were thoroughly, profoundly, comprehensively, and passionately rooted in Scripture.... Because of their importance—summarizing the Scriptures authoritatively and clarifying key points of confusion—the major creeds became reliable guides for what it meant to be Christian. That authority, in turn, is what has made them through the centuries so useful for so many purposes, including (in our own day) the purposes of Christian learning.[64]

The creeds are memorable and accessible summaries of the Christian faith. If the cultivation of a genuinely Christian worldview is the most valuable tool for academic and cultural engagement, and if forming a worldview involves clothing the teaching of Scripture into the lens through which the mind and heart see, then teaching the historic Christian creeds, first to our teachers and then to our students, may be the most strategic investment of time Christian schools and Christian families can make. Noll believes the greatest hope for Christian learning in our age is to "delve deeper into the

Christian faith itself. And going deeper into the Christian faith means, in the end, learning more of Jesus Christ."[65] Learning more of Jesus Christ is an essential component of Christian worldview formation.

THE VALUE OF OTHER SOURCES IN WORLDVIEW FORMATION

The special revelation of God in Scripture undoubtedly exerts the greatest influence on the formation of students' Christian worldview, but there are other sources rooted in the truth of God's general revelation. These include truth found in every academic discipline, discovered in creation and understood through human reason including philosophy and the study of human experience in history.[66] In these other influences there is value in students reading Christian books, learning about the contributions of Christian people, and acknowledging the role of the Christian church in the history of civilization. Christian worldviews are formed by wrestling with Christian ideas, while also comparing and contrasting ideas encountered in all subjects with Christian faith and understanding. This includes discussing ideas outside of class with all school personnel at school events, and when just hanging out with friends—anytime students wrestle with the way Christian truth engages with life and learning. All of these contribute to worldview formation.

WORLDVIEWS ARE FORMED NATURALLY AND SUPERNATURALLY

The process of Christian worldview formation is simultaneously natural and supernatural. The natural element comes from learning the truth of God's Word, reading Christian books, wrestling with Christian ideas, and learning the truth of God's world in a way that includes the truth we understand by reason informed by Christian faith. Christian ideas need not be forced into academic study in an artificial way but rather intentionally acknowledged in the myriad ways faith and learning cross paths. So much of learning in school and all of life is simply studying the wonders of the creation God has made while also identifying the many ways the world is not the way it is supposed to be due to the effects of the fall. At the same time, there are ways God has been working and is working through people to redeem all of creation and restore it to his intention at creation. The work of restoration anticipates the completion or consummation at the end of time. Creation, fall, redemption, and consummation are the themes woven throughout the fabric of learning in the Christian school and the shape of the garment of a Christian worldview.

Throughout this learning process, God is also at work supernaturally to superintend the process of worldview formation in students' hearts and minds. His Spirit is able to use truth from every source and illumine it to replace error, correct distortion, and apply it in ways that cause the lenses of students' minds and hearts to be shaped by it. This is the process of worldview formation. Naugle describes God's gracious and supernatural work in worldview formation this way:

> God can break into an individual's life, establish a beachhead in the heart, soften it to the truth of his Word, and save him or her by the power of the gospel of Jesus Christ through faith in him . . . The results of a transaction of this kind are wholly transformative in converting them to the worship of the true God and renewing their hearts and minds with truth. From a biblical perspective, therefore, the formation of a Christian worldview is ultimately a function of God's grace and redemption.[67]

With any means of grace—prayer, the sacraments, meditation, and spiritual reading—there is a natural context whereby the recipient cooperates with the source of grace through habitual, intentional, and disciplined exposure. The same is true in the formation of a Christian worldview. It requires the disciplined study of Scripture, reading of thoughtful Christian works, and receiving instruction from Christian people who have themselves wrestled, and are wrestling, with the ideas. The Christian-school mission to provide all instruction—teaching, coaching, and directing—from a Christian worldview adds great value to helping cultivate the students' Christian worldview.

CHRISTIAN WORLDVIEW FORMATION IN DAILY CLASSROOM INSTRUCTION

All children come to every type of school to learn the truth about the world in which they live through the study of the academic disciplines. The process of educating them involves instruction, discussion, reflection, practice, and teacher feedback. Daily lessons are designed to answer essential questions that are important for the students to understand. The children take tests, write papers, complete projects, and engage in other activities designed to help teachers evaluate and assess how well the students understand the subject at hand. Multiyear curricula present a scope and sequence of the knowledge and skills that school experts deem essential for students, which is then designed and presented to students in a spiral fashion; content is introduced in early grades, then amplified in future years. This is done not only because knowledge can be forgotten, but also because knowledge builds upon knowledge and students' level of understanding deepens as children mature. The cumulative effect of this ongoing process of education enables students to understand the truth about the world around them and prepares them to live better in accordance with it.

When I surveyed experienced and effective Christian-school teachers, I asked, "How, or in what ways, do teachers in Christian schools develop in their students a Christian worldview?" The most frequent response was that it happens through direct classroom instruction that connects to and integrates the academic content with the Christian faith, most often by approaching it through the lens of a Christian worldview. Here are some examples. In each one, the teacher integrates faith with learning by identifying a relationship or connection between the specific idea from the academic subject and what Scripture tells us about God's design for the world at creation, the distortion brought by the fall, the way all of creation is being redeemed to his purpose and intent at creation, and the hopeful destiny of complete restoration at the consummation of all things. Sometimes the connection is directly to a Bible verse but most often the connection is to the teaching of the broad themes of Scripture clothed in the concept of worldview. The teachers' ability to identify and make these connections in daily instruction is a specialized skill, one that is cultivated over time and intentionally planned into the essential questions and assessments in daily lessons. Look for the connections in these various responses:

> High School Humanities
> Every public high school English teacher teaching a unit on *Oedipus Rex* may require students to write an exam essay answering the question, How are the problems of determinism, divine sovereignty, and personal responsibility presented in Sophocles's *Oedipus Rex*? But in her Christian school, my daughter was asked to write an exam answering this question: How do the writings of C. S. Lewis [a Christian author] and Alvin Plantinga [a Christian philosopher] provide us with a resolution of the problem of determinism, divine sovereignty, and personal responsibility as presented in Sophocles's *Oedipus Rex*?

High School American Literature

When we read *The Scarlet Letter*, our essential question is how should the church respond when one of us sins big time? Hawthorne, being quite critical of his Puritan ancestors, answers by saying, "Not like they did!" We explore the author's criticism of the church and consider where his criticism might have been correct. What kind of man is Dimmesdale, for example? What kind of Christian leader? How might we apply these same criticisms to today's church? In what ways are we sometimes hypocritical? What is the difference between a hypocrite and a Christian who struggles with sin? Along with studying this novel as a piece of literature, we have the freedom to discuss worldview.

High School History

In the field of history, every culture, every movement, every artistic accomplishment reflects certain worldview pictures of human nature. The Scriptures also teach things about human nature. If we ask students to explain what the Jacobins in the French Revolution understood about human nature, we can ask how those views worked out in the actions the Jacobins took. We can then compare and contrast that with our own applications of our Christian understanding of human nature.

High School Business

These are several of the essential questions that form the core of our high school business class:

1. Our work is intended to glorify God, protect and improve creation, and work toward the renewal of all things. How does the Christian worldview guide your work?
2. How do we develop sustainable opportunities for people to thrive and flourish? It is not enough to produce a good that people will buy. We must create products that improve the lives of the end users.

Middle-School History

We look at how human nature impacts the design of governments. How does it undermine or support the success of communism and capitalism?

Fourth-Grade History

What drove the Pilgrims to take the massive risk of leaving England for the New World? How does the US Constitution allow for the freedom to practice religion, and what is the impact on the church in places where governments do not make provisions to allow for this freedom?

Second-Grade Study of Greece and Rome
A question I ask my students in our study of Greece and Rome is, in what ways might the Olympics look similar and different if they were designed in every way to be Christian?

In our study of Greek myths we learn that the Greeks had many gods, each with a different realm of responsibility and attribute. Iris is the goddess of the rainbow, and Poseidon is the god of the sea. We compare and contrast these with the one true God of the Bible who created the rainbow and has the power to control the sea.

We also note how Alexander the Great spread the Greek language throughout Asia as he conquered nations. Three hundred years later we see the impact of Alexander's conquests and how God controls the events of history, as the writers of the New Testament wrote in Greek as the language of the people.

We also compare and contrast Cyrus the Great with King David of Israel. We look at the characteristics of great kings in ancient times and today, while considering how God praised David as a "man after his own heart."

Kindergarten Science
In our unit on plants, we look at the way God designed seeds to grow. But even when soil, water, and sun are present, God still provides a force that causes things to grow. As we learn about photosynthesis, we see how God made humans and animals to exhale carbon dioxide that plants use, and plants send out oxygen that humans and animals need. These show how God designed creation and provides for its needs.

We also see how God created all things to need a time or season of rest, recovery, and preparation like trees going dormant, animals hibernating, and our bodies needing sleep, and a Sabbath day.

Elementary School Phonics
In our study of phonics we learn the history of the English language. Students learn that English words come from many linguistic sources, and we talk about how the Tower of Babel impacted the spread of many languages in the world.

Elementary School Geography
While learning the locations and capitals of Asian nations, we also learn about their main religions. We also talk about God's love for

the eight billion people of the world and pray for the people in these nations that God will bring the truth of the gospel to them.

Elementary School Science
When we study the human body we constantly marvel at how extraordinary and complex the body is. Often every student can think of a different amazing fact, illustrating our memory verse from Psalm 139 that we are "fearfully and wonderfully made."

Elementary School Grammar
In our study of grammar we see how important it is because God chose to communicate his Word to us in writing (not movies or videos). This adds value to our efforts to understand the power of words and how to write clearly to communicate well.

Elementary School Mathematics
Our lesson looked at symmetrical lines. As we looked more deeply at the idea of symmetry in creation, I had the students come to the front of the class; we identified ways we see and reflect symmetry: two eyes, ears, etc. We looked also at symmetry in the rest of creation and concluded that since God built symmetry into the design of creation, we find it pleasing when we see it in many aspects of our lives as well.

Kindergarten Reading
As we read a book, we always reflect on the behaviors and decisions of the characters, asking if what they did was right and admirable. When we do this, we make connections to our Bible lessons on Jesus and his teachings.

Elementary School Art
As we look at the elements of design and color, we look at how creative God is in designing the different kinds, colors, and shapes of birds, flowers, trees, and leaves, and we imagine how different life might be without these.

I provide these examples to help readers glimpse the cumulative impact of instruction, day after day, subject after subject, year after year, upon helping shape the lenses of students' minds and hearts so they see the world in a clear, complete, unified, and cohesive way. This natural and supernatural process of Christian worldview formation prepares students for future study and opens doors to a deeper academic and cultural analysis from a defensible faith.

THE FUNCTION OF A WORLDVIEW: ACADEMIC AND CULTURAL ANALYSIS

The Christian-school mission of worldview formation prepares students for the world of ideas they will encounter in college or after college in culture. We've already considered the all-too-common example of the Christian-school student going off to biology class at the state university or private college entirely unprepared for the inundation of data, knowledge, and theory presented from an unfamiliar worldview. This often creates a crisis of faith, where she believes she faces an either/or question: do I believe the faith in which I was raised, or do I believe what I am now being taught? The crisis—and what seems to be a stark option—is the result of being unfamiliar with the data of science and the naturalist worldview dominant in the field of science and throughout American colleges and universities. It is difficult for Christians attending such colleges not to be influenced by the power, overt or insidious, of ideas and worldviews that may be radically opposed to Christian faith. Students must be prepared by having formed their own Christian worldviews and understanding how to identify ideas reflecting different worldviews and how to engage them.

The challenge for Christian college students to construct a Christian worldview is even greater, especially in schools not intentionally Christian, considering that individual academic disciplines are often dominated by a particular worldview that is hostile to Christian faith. Harris recounts the institutional peer pressure felt by Paul Vitz who, having been raised in the Christian faith, became an atheist in college before returning to belief years later. Vitz explained a major reason for his becoming an atheist:

> I desired to be accepted by the powerful and influential scientists in the field of psychology. In particular, I wanted to be accepted by my professors in graduate school. As a graduate student, I was thoroughly socialized by the specific "culture" of academic research psychology. My professors at Stanford University, however much they might disagree among themselves on psychological theory, were, as far as I could tell, united in two things: their intense career ambitions and their rejection of religion.[68]

Psychology is certainly not the only academic discipline pervaded by specific or implicit assumptions and ideas that are diametrically opposed to Christian theism. Atheistic naturalism is by far the most dominant as no academic discipline takes as its starting point the living God who created all realities.

Because of the worldviews pervading the academic disciplines that are in conflict with Christian faith, even students in Christian colleges must be alert and prepared for worldview conflict when immersed in academic study. Today it is increasingly common and strategic for students to consider a gap year between high school and college to pursue experiences to help solidify what they believe and ground them further in Christian thought.

Our children, and the students in Christian schools, must be prepared to recognize ideas that are patently absurd and unsubstantiated by data and be able to identify the *a priori*—assumed to be true without evidence— commitments. Students who enter college unprepared to do so may accept the idea without engaging and wrestling with it from a Christian worldview, asking, is it true? Does it correspond to the way things really are? If it is true, how does it fit into a cohesive understanding of all truth in a way that expands the students' knowledge of the universe? If it is not true, what data from their unified understanding of the truth of God's Word and world does it contradict? If its veracity is uncertain, what resource—people, books, research—might the students consult to explore it?

Christian students at every level are like people constantly working a giant puzzle that, fully assembled, forms a complete and cohesive picture of all created realities—all truth—of the world in which they live. Christian students who simply accept ideas without engaging and wrestling with them from a Christian worldview acquire puzzle pieces that are impossible to fit in the picture they are assembling. Adding more and more pieces that don't fit undermines the work of assembly, causes frustration, and can lead to crises of faith. I've seen students founder rather than flourish as they seek to engage the academic disciplines and all of culture in a way that advances truth from a defensible Christian faith.

THE VALUE OF CHRISTIAN WORLDVIEW INTEGRATED INSTRUCTION

The best preparation for encountering false ideas is knowing what is true. Many students are able to get fine academic training in schools absent any unifying worldview and replete with often-conflicting worldviews. And many Christian students participate in church youth groups and valuable parachurch ministries that help nurture students' faith commitment.

There are even some valuable intensive ministries that focus on the concept of worldview. But nothing prepares students to engage ideas from a wide variety of worldviews better than daily instruction, year after year, from Christian teachers who have mastered their academic content, have received best-practices teacher training, and are prepared to cultivate students' Christian worldviews through intentional instruction from a Christian worldview. This is what defines the distinctive mission of Christian schooling and an indispensable part of its life-shaping value.

CHAPTER SUMMARY

The goal of worldview formation is entirely distinctive to the Christian school. A Christian worldview has a definite shape and reflects the overarching themes of Scripture and its four pillars: creation, fall, redemption, and consummation. The Bible is the primary source of a worldview requiring students to have a thorough understanding of the Bible, and the historic creeds may be valuable tools for learning Christian truth today. Christian literature and other sources from God's general revelation in creation also contribute to worldview formation. Worldviews are created naturally and supernaturally, through disciplined study and reflection as well as the gracious work of God's Spirit applying truth to students' hearts and minds. The most valuable tool for worldview formation is daily classroom instruction in the academic subjects from a distinctly Christian worldview. This shapes students' hearts and minds to see the world in a clear and unified way while preparing them for deeper academic and cultural analysis from a defensible faith in college and flourishing in life.

We turn now to the aspect of the Christian-school mission that is shared by the Christian home, church, and parachurch organizations such as Young Life, Cru, the Fellowship of Christian Athletes, and others.

7

Authentic Spiritual Formation

What It Is, What It Isn't, and How It Happens

"If Christian families, churches, and schools are not intentional about helping students understand the difference between the external self-righteousness of the Pharisees and authentic righteousness that comes by faith in Christ through the work of the Holy Spirit in the heart, they may inadvertently contribute to, or even promote and celebrate, the formation of a fraudulent spiritual foundation that will fail."

—TOM STONER

"Nonetheless, this is academic evangelism at its best—the Gospel made appealing by its ability to meet the mind's as well as the soul's deepest needs. Done properly, by teachers who know both their subject and the gospel, it is perhaps the most satisfying marriage of spiritual and academic purposes.

—RICHARD RIESEN

Instruction in All Academic Subjects	Instruction from a Christian Worldview	Nurturing Christian Faith & Character
↓	↓	↓
Academic Formation	Christian Worldview Formation	Spiritual Formation

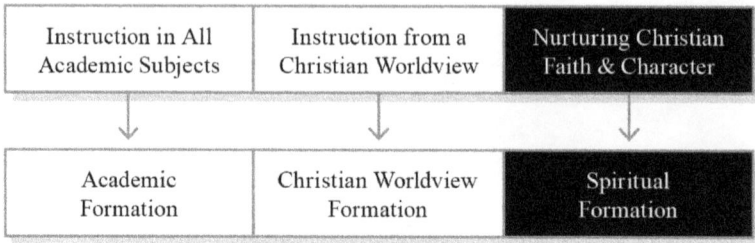

The Mission of Spiritual Formation

The third element in the threefold mission of Christian schooling is *spiritual formation,* or the process of learning and growth that intends to engender and deepen Christian faith and the character that flows from faith. Christian people—parents, grandparents, and caregivers—value it highly, recognizing just how essential this is for the child they love to flourish in the future. In the work of spiritual formation of students, the mission of the Christian school is a partner whenever possible with the Christian home, the educational mission of the church Sunday school, church youth group, and parachurch organizations such as Young Life and the Fellowship of Christian Athletes, among others. Spiritual formation is so central to the mission of Christian schooling that it often is expressed in school mission statements:

> *Anytown* Christian School is an independent day school that offers a college preparatory education based on biblical values that equips students to be lifetime followers of Jesus Christ.

As we have noted, the very idea of a Christian school, and what defines its place in the private-school marketplace, is its mission to provide an educational option that is consistent with parents' deeply held convictions of faith and thus a welcome partner with the Christian home and church in passing this faith on to children.

Before we look more closely at how spiritual formation takes place in the context of a Christian school, we answer a more basic question: What does spiritual formation look like? In other words, if a student is spiritually formed, what is the result?

UNDERSTANDING THE CHRISTIAN FAITH

The first major aspect of spiritual formation is the intentional process by which all the personnel at the Christian school, together with the home and church whenever possible, help students understand the Christian faith—what Christians believe. As students grow in their understanding of the truth of Christian faith, the goal and hope is that they, too, will believe in the gospel of Jesus Christ, be restored to a personal relationship with God, and receive new life, eternal life, from the Spirit.

Spiritual formation is essential to human flourishing. Being all we were created to be requires a restored personal relationship with God that he intended at creation. The opening chapters of Genesis give us a glimpse of the personal relationship Adam and Eve enjoyed with God, free from shame and characterized by peace. The same was true of their relationship with each other. Their sin changed everything. Because God is holy, their sin—and after them the sin of all people—fractured their relationship with God and caused interpersonal strife. Right there, at the very moment of Adam and Eve's sin against God, we see that God does not treat his people as their sins deserve, for he is a God of grace and mercy. God so deeply desires a personal relationship with the people he created that he immediately promised to provide a remedy, a Savior.

To pay the penalty of sin for the human race, the promised Savior needed to be born into the human race in a particular place, time, and people group. God chose a man named Abram and established a special covenant relationship with him. God told him to leave his homeland and go to the land he would show him, promising, "I will make you into a great nation and I will bless you; . . . and all peoples on earth will be blessed through you" (Genesis 12:2–3). God changed Abram's name to Abraham, meaning "father of many people," and his descendants became the nation of Israel. Jesus Christ, a descendant of Abraham, is God's promised Savior. He was with God at the creation of the world, and he was born as a baby—fully God and fully human—in Bethlehem, in the land of Israel. For the sake of restoring us to relationship with God, he lived a sinless life, died on the cross as our substitute, paying the price for the sin of Adam and Eve—our sin—then rose victorious over death.

On the basis of his sinless life, death, and resurrection, Jesus now freely offers a restored relationship with God to anyone who believes: "If you declare with your mouth, 'Jesus is Lord,' and believe in your heart that God raised him from the dead, you will be saved" (Romans 10:9). At the

83

moment of faith in Christ, the Holy Spirit enters the individual's heart, resulting in spiritual life or new life through the Spirit. This moment is what theologians call "conversion" and what Jesus refers to when he tells Nicodemus, "Very truly I tell you, no one can see the kingdom of God unless they are born again" (John 3:3). The presence of the Holy Spirit restores the personal relationship, resulting in peace with God, and assures the hope of eternal life after death. "Therefore, since we have been justified through faith, we have peace with God through our Lord Jesus Christ, through whom we have gained access by faith into this grace in which we now stand. And we boast in the hope of the glory of God" (Romans 5:1–2). In his autobiography *Confessions*, St. Augustine's search for truth took him through numerous philosophies before he came to faith in Jesus Christ and famously said: "You stir man to take pleasure in praising you, because you have made us for yourself, and our heart is restless until it rests in you."[69]

The starting place for genuine spiritual formation in students' lives is understanding Christian faith—what Christians believe, and believing for themselves resulting in conversion, spiritual birth, and hearts at peace with God.

RESPONDING FAITHFULLY WITH LOVE AND OBEDIENCE

Spiritual formation only begins with personal conversion to faith in Jesus Christ. A second major aspect of spiritual formation, which is an indispensable outworking of what it means to believe, is the intentional process by which students come to understand that faith in Christ demands a response of love for God expressed primarily by obedience to his commands. All the commands of Scripture paint a picture of this response of love and how God intends for his people to live in relationship with him and others.

> We love because he first loved us. (1 John 4:19)

> Therefore, I urge you, brothers and sisters, in view of God's mercy, to offer your bodies as a living sacrifice. (Romans 12:1)

> In fact, this is love for God: to keep his commands. And his commands are not burdensome. (1 John 5:3)

Jesus replied: "'Love the Lord your God with all your heart and with all your soul and with all your mind.' This is the first and greatest commandment. And the second is like it: 'Love your neighbor as yourself.' All the Law and the Prophets hang on these two commandments." (Matthew 22:37–40)

The order of God's loving action followed by our response of loving obedience is critical to spiritual formation. Many people mistakenly view the Ten Commandments as actions one must do to earn a relationship with God when they, too, begin with God's loving actions toward his chosen people of Israel. "I am the Lord your God, who brought you out of Egypt, out of the land of slavery. You shall have no other gods before me" (Exodus 20:2–3). It is very common, in fact it is the natural "default wiring" of the human heart, to reverse the order from God's actions prompting our response to our actions attempting to promote God's response. This reversal is fraudulent and toxic to authentic spiritual formation.

The very moment we believe by faith, the Holy Spirit begins the process of renewing our minds to help us understand and conform our thinking to the truth revealed in creation and Scripture, as well as the process of renewing our hearts to love what is good and hate what is evil. Theologians call the process sanctification. Christian author Frederick Buechner calls it "the gradual transformation of a sow's ear into a silk purse."[70]

The lifelong process of sanctification involves growing in righteousness to become more and more like Jesus in the ways we think, the words we speak, and the actions we do. This transformation is accomplished by God's power through the Holy Spirit. We are no more able to change ourselves to become like Christ than we are able to save ourselves from our sin in the first place. It is Jesus Christ who saves us, and it is the Holy Spirit of Christ who transforms us to be the people he created us to be. Our job in salvation and sanctification is to believe, for our relationship with God is by faith from start to finish. Inherent in believing is cooperating with the work of the Spirit in our hearts: "Since we live by the Spirit, let us keep in step with the Spirit" (Galatians 5:25) and not resisting his restorative work in our lives. When we die, or when Christ returns at the end of time, we will no longer need faith, for we will see God face to face.

So far, we have provided a two-part answer to the question, what does spiritual formation look like? First, it looks like faith formation or the process by which students come to believe in the gospel of Jesus Christ resulting in personal faith and conversion. Second, it looks like Christian character formation or the process by which students understand that faith in Christ demands a response of love for God expressed primarily by obedience to his commands. The result of this lifelong process is transformation into the image of Jesus Christ. This image is what we mean by being all we are capable of being and the people God created us to be.

I am tempted at this stage to go on to describe the practical ways that Christian schools contribute to the work of spiritual formation. However, I would be leaving out a crucial challenge to the work of spiritual formation that may be best illustrated by a personal example.

BUILDING ON A FAULTY SPIRITUAL FOUNDATION

I would not trade my years at my Christian high school for anything. I loved it. It helped shape who I am and influenced my career. The older I get, the more I value my experience. With the benefit of more than thirty years' hindsight, however, I realize that when I started as a freshman, the foundation of my spiritual life was faulty and I was about to shift into high gear and work overtime to build a spiritual house upon it.

Like so many of the students in Christian schools, I was raised in a Christian home and in a very good church. So as is often the case with this profile, I never remember not believing in God. I do remember asking God to come into my heart as my Savior weekly for a significant portion of my childhood—just to be certain that it took. When I prayed to trust Jesus Christ as my Savior, I recognized that I could not save myself; I needed Jesus, and I believed the essential truth of the gospel of Jesus Christ: Christ died for me.

However, my world—my Christian home, my Christian church, and the Christian culture in which I was raised—was so filled with messages, audible and inaudible, communicating the expectations of what a Christian does (read the Bible, obey parents, pray, perform acts of service, tithe my allowance . . .) and does not do (lie, cheat, steal, and the list goes on), that it seemed clear to me that the rightness of my relationship with God was dictated by my actions. If I did well meeting the expectations placed upon me, I was confident that I was doing well as a Christian. At times when I was slacking off in my efforts at daily devotions, prayer, service, and other acts of piety, or when I sinned by making a mistake, I felt guilty that I was not a very good Christian.

Armed with this as my understanding of the Christian life, I enrolled at the Christian school, where I found opportunity after opportunity to get involved in worthy causes to which I was drawn like a magnet. From my perspective, the opportunities of discipleship groups, student leadership, speaking in chapel, and leading Bible studies were spiritual résumé builders and sources of spiritual pride to commend myself to a God of high expectations and endless commands. Through it all, I managed to find in all my efforts a personal identity that was often affirmed and celebrated by so many around me.

Having begun with the recognition that I could not save myself and needed Jesus and what he did on the cross, when it came to my response of love for God expressed in obedience to his commands, I believed it was somehow my job; seeing no other choice, I worked feverishly to conform my actions to all God's commandments and expectations. I figured "if a little is good, a lot must be better," so the more Bible reading, prayer, and service I could do, the better. It meant I could better conform myself to the image of the great people of faith I read about. Talk about a tough row to hoe and a huge burden to carry on my own. The only consolation I found as I strained under the load was the praise of others, which provided a trickle of approval for my dry heart.

I remember being baffled by passages like John 15, where Jesus says, "I am the vine; you are the branches. If you remain in me and I in you, you will bear much fruit; apart from me you can do nothing." I was confused. What does it mean, "you can do nothing"? On a mission trip in college to Romania, I asked a dear Romanian friend, "How can I become the man God wants me to be?" He responded, "First of all, let God do it, because he will do a better job." I nodded and smiled but in my brain, his words produced an error message: "does not compute." What did he mean?

THE WINDS OF CHANGE

After college I volunteered at a Christ-centered residential community in New Hampshire, where adults with life-controlling problems and pain came to heal and learn about the God who made them. One cold, early spring day, it was raining so hard they very uncharacteristically called us indoors (from harvesting firewood) for an impromptu Bible study. We sat in a group, soaked to the bone, grateful to be indoors, as we turned our attention to something God had to say in his Word.

The study leader had us turn to the Beatitudes in Matthew 5. "Blessed are the poor in spirit, for theirs is the kingdom of heaven." He explained that the word for *poor* meant "bankrupt." As I remember it, he said, "Jesus started his teaching by saying those who are blessed or find favor in God's eyes are the spiritually bankrupt, for to them belongs the kingdom of God." It was as if neon lights flashed and sirens blared in my mind: "This is important for you, Tom." This moment initiated a change in my thinking about the foundation of my relationship to God, particularly as it relates to how I obey his commands. This moment also led directly to another watershed moment.

More than ten years later, in the midst of the myriad joys and challenges of life, work, and family, I was overwhelmingly aware of all God's scriptural commands—the way he desired me to live in thought, word, and deed—and the many ways I fell short. I'd felt this way many times before. What was new, however, was my awareness and deep conviction that there was no way I could ever get myself to the place where I met God's expectations.

Arriving home late that night, I threw my keys on the couch and said out loud: "I can't do it!" No sooner had the words come out of my mouth but I heard what I am certain was the voice of the Holy Spirit in my heart: "It's about time. I've been trying to get you to realize that for a long time." My heart flooded with a very deep peace, love, and acceptance. The moment I admitted my utter failure and inability to meet the demands of God's law, I experienced God's grace, and I finally understood the essential truth of the gospel of Jesus Christ that had escaped me for so long: "I can't; he can."[71] This new awareness opened a door for me to relate to God in a new way—the only authentic way, as one who is weak and needy to the One who knows our weakness and has met them all in the person and work of Jesus Christ.

SELF-RIGHTEOUSNESS AS A SPIRITUAL FOUNDATION: RARE OR COMMON?

The attitudes and actions of the first-century Pharisees paint a picture of the fraudulent spiritual formation we have been exploring. Consider Jesus's parable about the Pharisee and the tax collector. Notice Jesus's intended audience:

To some who were confident of their own righteousness and looked down on everybody else, Jesus told this parable: "Two men went up to the temple to pray, one a Pharisee and the other a tax collector. The Pharisee stood by himself and prayed: 'God, I thank you that I am not like other people—robbers, evildoers, adulterers—or even like this tax collector. I fast twice a week and give a tenth of all I get.'

"But the tax collector stood at a distance. He would not even look up to heaven, but beat his breast and said, 'God, have mercy on me, a sinner.'

"I tell you that this man, rather than the other, went home justified before God. For all those who exalt themselves will be humbled, and those who humble themselves will be exalted." (Luke 18:9–14)

The posture of the tax collector reflects the foundation of his relationship with God. He stands at a distance, does not look up, and beats his breast and cries to God for mercy. I cannot imagine a clearer picture of the message of the gospel—"I can't; he can"—than the tax collector in this parable. Jesus confirms that the tax collector went home in right relationship with a holy God on the basis of his humble cry for mercy.

The posture of the Pharisee also reflects the foundation of his relationship with God. He stands, prays about himself, thanking God that he is not like other people, then commends himself to God, and anyone listening, for his superior personal morality and outward acts of piety. The Pharisees throughout the Gospels are examples of fraudulent spirituality often referred to as *legalism*, or those whose relationship with God is based upon their efforts to keep God's laws by what they do and do not do—visible acts of piety and sins. Like a plastic banana, they look real on the outside, but Jesus confirms that the Pharisee did not go home justified or in right standing with God.

RELYING ON THE SPIRIT FOR TRANSFORMATION

The first aspect of spiritual formation is the intentional process of helping students to understand the Christian faith, anticipating that personal understanding is essential to personal conversion to faith in the gospel of Jesus Christ. The second aspect is the intentional process by which students come to understand that faith in Christ demands a response of love for God expressed primarily by obedience to his commands, which describe God's intention at creation for the way he intended people to live in relationship with him. Jesus Christ is the perfect representation of God's law. The third essential aspect of spiritual formation addresses how, or by what process, a Christian's mind and heart are changed from the way he or she naturally is at the time of first belief to being made new to reflect the image of Jesus Christ.

This question is the central theme of all of Scripture: how does God's plan of redemption in Jesus Christ restore people to relationship with God and in doing so restore their minds and hearts from the effects of sin? It is no coincidence that the Pharisees' interactions with Jesus are featured prominently in the Gospels, and then God chose a Pharisee (Philippians 3:5), named Saul, to show us, and then teach us in his New Testament letters, the answer to the question we are now asking.

As a result of Adam and Eve's sin, every person—the entire human race—is born with a "sinful" or an "old" nature that is inclined to think and act in ways contrary to God's laws and what God desires. The apostle Paul lists the common actions that result from our sinful nature: "The acts of the sinful nature are obvious: sexual immorality, impurity and debauchery; idolatry and witchcraft; hatred, discord, jealousy, fits of rage, selfish ambition, dissensions, factions and envy; drunkenness, orgies, and the like. I warn you, as I did before, that those who live like this will not inherit the kingdom of God" (Galatians 5:19–21).

We are born unable to understand the life of flourishing God has in mind for us in relationship with him, with hard hearts and strong wills that desire to fulfill our natural inclinations. When we come to faith in Christ, these patterns of thinking, speaking, and acting are not immediately annihilated (do I hear an Amen?); rather, they remain eager to express themselves as they have done our whole lives. However, what does immediately change is the new presence and new power of the Holy Spirit. The new birth of the Spirit breaking into the heart leads to repentance or a change of mind toward God that enables one to see who Christ is and understand the truth of the gospel. In the light of this truth, one's heart is also changed, resulting in love for God and others. The Holy Spirit immediately begins the lifelong work of completely renewing the mind and heart and changing (transforming) all the deeply ingrained, natural patterns from one's old nature. The result is growth toward reflecting in ever-increasing measure God's image in and through the unique individual God created one to be.

If the Holy Spirit encountered no resistance to this work of transformation, I imagine this process would be less difficult and be completed in much less time. However, the Holy Spirit does encounter resistance from the old patterns of thinking, speaking, and acting. Paul says, "For the flesh [sinful nature] desires what is contrary to the Spirit, and the Spirit what is contrary to the flesh. They are in conflict with each other, so that you are not to do whatever you want" (Galatians 5:17).[72] The work of the Holy Spirit encounters further opposition from a fallen and broken world that peddles ideas, goods, and opportunities that are accompanied by a lie, from the father of lies and enemy of our souls, that the world and its desires will satisfy the mind's deepest questions and the heart's deepest needs.

This brings us directly to the question: how, or by what power, are we made new? This is the third, essential part of what spiritual formation looks like from its inception to maturity. The answer we long for our children and students to understand is that the heart is made new only by the power of the Holy Spirit. The apostle Paul writes:

> Since you have heard about Jesus and have learned the truth that comes from him, throw off your old sinful nature and your former way of life, which is corrupted by lust and deception. Instead, let the Spirit renew your thoughts and attitudes. Put on your new nature, created to be like God—truly righteous and holy. (Ephesians 4:21–24 NLT)

> Therefore, I urge you, brothers and sisters, in view of God's mercy, to offer your bodies as living sacrifices, holy and pleasing to God—this is your true and proper worship. Do not conform to the pattern of this world, but be transformed by the renewing of your mind. Then you will be able to test and approve what God's will is—his good, pleasing and perfect will. (Romans 12:1–2)

The Holy Spirit renews our hearts. Our job is to cooperate, not resist, and keep in step with his work: "Since we live by the Spirit, let us keep in step with the Spirit" (Galatians 5:25). The lifelong work of changing our hearts and minds is done by God through the power of the Holy Spirit and the evidence of this transforming work in our hearts is an ever-increasing measure of the fruit of the Spirit: "love, joy, peace, patience, kindness, goodness, faithfulness, gentleness, and self-control" (Galatians 5:22–23).[73] This fruit, rather than public piety or even displays of personal morality, is the most powerful witness to the reality of Christ in our lives and the truth of Christian faith. Our work of spiritual formation will identify this as the target for our students.

What is the other option? If not the Holy Spirit, how else would we be made righteous so that we meet the expectations of God's commandments and laws? There is no other real option, only a fraudulent one that attempts to meet the demands of God's laws by our own efforts. This is the path chosen by the Pharisees. It is also the path that fits perfectly with the default wiring and natural inclinations of our hearts, rooted in sinful pride and the path I inadvertently traveled for many years. We have a natural bent or curvature to our souls, which resists the truth that we are weak and humbly dependent upon God. And we have an unusual capacity to deceive ourselves into thinking we're doing better than we actually are and that we *can* do it. Paul chides his readers: "You foolish Galatians! Who has bewitched you? Before your very eyes Jesus Christ was clearly portrayed as crucified. I would like to learn just one thing from you: Did you receive the Spirit by the works of the law, or by believing what you heard? Are you so foolish? After beginning by means of the Spirit, are you now trying to finish by means of the flesh?" (Galatians 3:1–3). However, the goodness and love of God causes the Holy Spirit of truth to persist in helping us understand that we are unable to do it ourselves, so that by his power he can complete his work.

AN ILLUSTRATION FROM *THE PILGRIM'S PROGRESS*

There is a profoundly simple illustration of this essential idea for spiritual formation in John Bunyan's classic allegory *The Pilgrim's Progress*. In the opening pages of the book, Christian leaves his home in the city of destruction at the direction of Evangelist, to begin his journey on the narrow way to the Celestial City. Christian carries a heavy burden on his back from the guilt and shame of his sin. One of the first people Christian meets on his journey is Mr. Worldly Wiseman from the great town of Carnal Policy, very near the town of Christian's home. Seeing the heavy burden on Christian's back, Mr. Worldly Wiseman advises him to "with all speed get thyself rid of thy Burden" for he will never have peace of mind or enjoy the Blessing God has given him until he rids himself of the burden. Christian responds:

> That is that which I seek for, even to be rid of this heavy Burden;
> but get it off myself, I cannot: Nor is there a Man in our country,

that can take it off my shoulders; therefore I am going this Way, as I told you, that I may be rid of my Burden.[74]

Soon Christian is shown a fire that burns hotter despite the water thrown on it by the devil, and he is told the fire is the Work of Grace in the heart. When Christian is shown the way to the Cross, he runs to it. When he sees the cross, his burden is released, he sees it no more, and he leaps for joy. Bunyan shows the source of power for the Christian life from start to finish, for salvation and sanctification, comes not from ourselves but from God. It is a work of his grace, by the cross, and through the ongoing work of his Spirit in our hearts.

THE MISSION OF SPIRITUAL FORMATION IN CHRISTIAN SCHOOLS

The profile of the typical Christian-school student is similar to mine—decades ago. Many or even most kids come from Christian homes and attend church where they have been taught from the time they were born what is right and wrong and what God wants them to do and not do; most have done their best to comply. The opportunity to be raised in a Christian home, church, and school is a blessing from God.

This profile, however, lends itself to a spiritual foundation that glosses over or misses altogether the grace of God in Jesus Christ and resembles the self-righteous efforts of the Pharisees, who believe that all the good things they do will earn God's favor. The very act of going to a Christian school can be a source of spiritual pride, along with the emphasis on doing acts of personal piety (e.g., devotions, prayer, mission trips, service projects) and not doing acts of immorality (e.g., drinking, sex, drugs, dancing). If a Christian school, as well as the home, church, or Christian ministry, is not intentional about teaching students the difference between the self-righteousness of the Pharisees and authentic righteousness that comes by faith in Christ through the work of the Holy Spirit in the heart, they may inadvertently contribute to, or even promote and celebrate, the formation of a fraudulent spiritual foundation.

In the Sermon on the Mount, Jesus focuses the expected standard of true righteousness far deeper than external actions, such as murder or adultery: "But I tell you that anyone who is angry with his brother will be subject to judgment" and "anyone who looks at a woman lustfully has already committed adultery with her in his heart" (Matthew 5:22, 28). Jesus is not merely using hyperbole; true righteousness is righteousness of the heart through the Spirit. Against this standard, the only honest response of every person alive is "that is impossible; I could never meet that standard." That is precisely the confession of anyone who understands the simple truth of the gospel of Jesus Christ—"I can't; he can"—and the only true foundation for a relationship with God. Any other foundation will fail.

It will fail when the inevitable storms and challenges of life cause it to collapse like the house built upon the sand.[75] Perhaps the most common scenario involves the students who get tired of performance-based acceptance from trying to do everything they believe to be expected of them from family, church, and God, and they simply walk away. They may think they are walking away from the Christian faith, but they are really walking away from the Christian works; they never truly understood the love of God who accepts us as we are: weak and in need of his grace. The distorted system of legalism they were taught and exposed to is partly to blame for their disillusionment.

An improper spiritual foundation fails to cultivate the mind and nourish the soul in ways that lead to growth, maturity, and the beauty of true righteousness witnessed by others as the fruit of the Spirit's work. This vitality enables the Christian to engage with others in the various arenas of life with a robust witness to a cohesive understanding of all truth that is compelling, defensible, and winsome—salt and light in a dark and broken world.

Most tragic of all, and a terrifyingly real consequence of a fraudulent spiritual foundation, are the people who believe themselves to be righteous on the basis of the things they appeared to do in God's name, only to find out when it is too late that they never experienced the new birth of the Spirit in their hearts by faith and will remain apart from God for eternity.[76] In the light of this potential eternal reality, the stakes of authentic spiritual formation in our homes, churches, and schools could not be higher.

SPIRITUAL FORMATION THROUGH ACADEMIC INSTRUCTION

Christian schools have a tremendous opportunity seven hours a day to combine their personnel and program in the intentional process of spiritual formation. How exactly does spiritual formation contribute to the whole mix?

The Christian school participates in spiritual formation through formal academic instruction in two ways. First, Christian schools teach Bible in addition to all the other subjects in their academic programs. From prekindergarten all the way through grade twelve, Christian schools design and teach a scope and sequence that typically begins with Bible characters and events, continues with surveys of the Old and New Testaments, and builds to courses that include systematic theology, biblical ethics, comparative religions, and alternative worldviews. Second, as we have noted, Christian schools teach all academic subjects from the unified perspective of a Christian worldview. Authors use expressions such as *academic evangelism* and the *evangelistic nature of truth* to refer to the distinctive mission of Christian schooling to nurture Christian faith by cultivating students' rational understanding of the truth of Christian faith combined with academic truth: "Nonetheless, this is academic evangelism at its best—the Gospel made appealing by its ability to meet the mind's as well as the soul's deepest needs. Done properly, by teachers who know both their subject and the gospel, it is perhaps the most satisfying marriage of spiritual and academic purposes."[77] Truth is powerful. As students come to understand how truth combines in a unified and cohesive view of all realities, this unity of the truth of all created realities presents a compelling case that God uses to draw students to personal faith.

In addition to classroom instruction, Christian schools are intentional about spiritual formation through weekly chapel services that include all-school worship, as well as testimonies of faith and Scripture-based messages presented by students, teachers, administrators, local youth pastors, and other guests. Some Christian schools employ a director of spiritual formation to coordinate a complete program of small groups, service projects, short-term mission experiences, and spiritual emphasis weeks, all designed to contribute to this important aspect of the Christian-school mission.

SPIRITUAL FORMATION AND THE PERSONAL RELATIONSHIPS WITH SCHOOL PERSONNEL

Students in Christian schools are surrounded by teachers, administrators, coaches, directors, and staff members who themselves have come to faith in Jesus Christ and are maturing in the character that flows from Christian faith. Most of these people have direct daily contact with students, and they are intentional about establishing personal relationships with them through which they can share their hearts and lives—including their faith. Our eighth-grade son came home talking about his PE teacher, who had shared his life story. He said, "Our jaws dropped," as the teacher talked about being a bully as a child because of his anger from a challenging home situation and then through tears shared how God had changed him through forgiveness and love. The power of such modeling comes from authenticity, providing students an example they can relate to and admire.

God often uses coaches and teachers to touch students' hearts and inspire in them a desire to be like a coach or teacher. One day at school, I saw a video on Twitter of one of our varsity football players getting baptized at his local church. As he professed his personal faith in Christ, he thanked his football coaches for all their support. I was thrilled for the student and to hear the shout-out to our football coaches. The next day I found the head football coach, told him that I had seen the video, and expressed my pride that the student gave a shout out to the football coaches. The coach responded, "Thank you. Yes, I know. I was there." The head coach was at the baptism along with other coaches and team players.

Finally, spiritual formation takes place in Christian schools similar to the way it takes place in the Christian home. In fact, *in loco parentis,* "in place of a parent," is a phrase commonly seen on Christian-school websites and refers to the ways parents invite the school to stand in for them during the school day. One of the most valuable ways this is true involves student discipline. The school and parents are aligned regarding the attitudes and actions they desire for the students to express in relationship with teachers, other students, the school community, and the local community. This alignment reflects their unified vision of flourishing rooted in Christian faith and the values of faith.

WHAT ABOUT STUDENTS WHO DON'T BELIEVE?

What about students who never come to faith or even who overtly reject Christian faith before they graduate from the Christian school? In terms of their spiritual formation, was their Christian-school experience wasted? By extension, we ask the same question about their time in a Christian home and church youth group. Was this a waste of time? Absolutely not.

The truth learned in Bible class and chapel, through worldview instruction integrated with the academic disciplines, and in the modeling of

God's grace in personal relationships with school personnel, added together with the truth learned in Sunday school, Sunday worship, youth group, and taught at home—all remains like dry kindling around the students' hearts and minds. At any future moment, the Holy Spirit is able to combine a spark with God's truth leading to personal faith and conversion. At that moment, the years of teaching in the home, church, and school ignite in a rush of reason to their minds and an expanded explosion of love for God in their hearts, making the investment of time and finances exceedingly strategic. The new spiritual life that results is essential to flourishing lives and prepares them to be fully alive—the people God made them to be.

WHAT ABOUT THE CALL FOR CHRISTIANS TO BE "SALT AND LIGHT" IN PUBLIC SCHOOLS?

Before closing this chapter, it may be valuable to comment on Jesus's call for Christians to be "salt and light" in a dark and needy world and the very real opportunity Christians have to be catalysts in the local public schools. Christian teachers have a powerful witness and impact in public schools as they model Christian faith as instruments of God's love to others. Many Christian families are also able to be salt and light in the local public schools as they build relationships with neighbors and other members of the local community through the shared experience of school life and events. Like teachers in schools, Christians who model lives changed by faith will have opportunities to share with others the hope they have in Christ. Public school communities are very strategic fields for Christian mission and churches.

The phrases "you are the salt of the earth" and "you are the light of the world" are from Jesus's first major teaching session with his disciples in what is known as the Sermon on the Mount, found in Matthew 5–7. This hillside teaching session was near the start of three very intensive years during which Jesus would spend all day every day helping his disciples understand the truth about who he was, the truth about the kingdom he came to establish, and the truth about events that would happen in the future. Jesus taught lessons, asked questions, told stories, performed miracles, and dialogued with the disciples as he nurtured their faith and understanding. One could say that Jesus's "salt and light" lesson was the start of a very intentional three-year intensive process of spiritual formation for his disciples directed by Jesus himself. After his death, resurrection, and ascension, some of the disciples lived for decades as salt and light in a very dark and needy world.

The most important consideration in all of this is how parents and caregivers will be intentional about ensuring a process of spiritual formation for their children throughout their school-aged years and how they might identify strategic partners in other families, their local church, and other Christian organizations. A good start in this process is understanding what spiritual formation looks like, how it is done, and why it is essential to prepare children to flourish in seventy-plus years of life, vocation, and Christian impact after college.

CHAPTER SUMMARY

Spiritual formation is the aspect of the Christian-school mission that is identical to the educational mission of the church Sunday school, the church youth group, and parachurch organizations such as Young Life and the Fellowship of Christian Athletes. There are three essential aspects of spiritual formation beginning with students understanding the Christian faith—what Christians believe—with the hope they will come to personal faith in Jesus Christ. This is followed by students recognizing that authentic faith demands a response of love for God expressed primarily by obedience to God's commands. Finally, students learn the only way their hearts and minds are renewed to become the people God made them to be is by the power of the Holy Spirit and not through their own efforts. Christian schools contribute to spiritual formation by including formal instruction in Bible and Christian theology in the standard curriculum and through what some authors call *academic evangelism* or classroom instruction that helps students see how Christian faith satisfies the deepest needs of their minds and souls. Christian-school personnel also contribute to spiritual formation by establishing personal relationships with students in which they model and share their own journeys of faith. Finally, teachers and school leaders operate in place of parents at school by sharing the attitudes and actions that are nurtured and disciplined throughout the day. The process of spiritual formation is an essential part of preparing students to flourish in their lives after they complete their schooling.

```
┌─────────────────────────────────────────────┐
│              Creator God                      │
│          Source of All Realities              │
└─────────────────────────────────────────────┘
                      ↓
┌─────────────────────────────────────────────┐
│                 Truth                         │
│          Corresponds to Reality               │
└─────────────────────────────────────────────┘
         ↓                         ↓
┌──────────────────────┐  ┌──────────────────────┐
│  Truth of God's World │  │  Truth of God's Word  │
│        Reason         │  │     Faith & Reason    │
└──────────────────────┘  └──────────────────────┘
         ↓                         ↓
┌──────────────┐              ┌──────────────┐
│   Academic   │ ← Disintegration →│  Christian │
│  Disciplines │              │     Faith    │
└──────────────┘              └──────────────┘
                 ┌─────────────────────────┐
                 │    Biblical Worldview    │ ←
                 └─────────────────────────┘
                      ↓   ↓   ↓
                 ┌─────────────────────────┐
              →  │   Academic Disciplines   │
                 └─────────────────────────┘
                           ↓
┌─────────────────────────────────────────────┐
│               Unity of Truth                  │
└─────────────────────────────────────────────┘
      ↓                ↓                ↓
┌──────────────┐ ┌──────────────┐ ┌──────────────┐
│Instruction in│ │Instruction   │ │Nurturing     │
│All Academic  │ │from a        │ │Christian     │
│Subjects      │ │Christian     │ │Faith &       │
│              │ │Worldview     │ │Character     │
└──────────────┘ └──────────────┘ └──────────────┘
      ↓                ↓                ↓
┌──────────────┐ ┌──────────────┐ ┌──────────────┐
│  Academic    │ │  Christian   │ │  Spiritual   │
│  Formation   │ │  Worldview   │ │  Formation   │
│              │ │  Formation   │ │              │
└──────────────┘ └──────────────┘ └──────────────┘
```

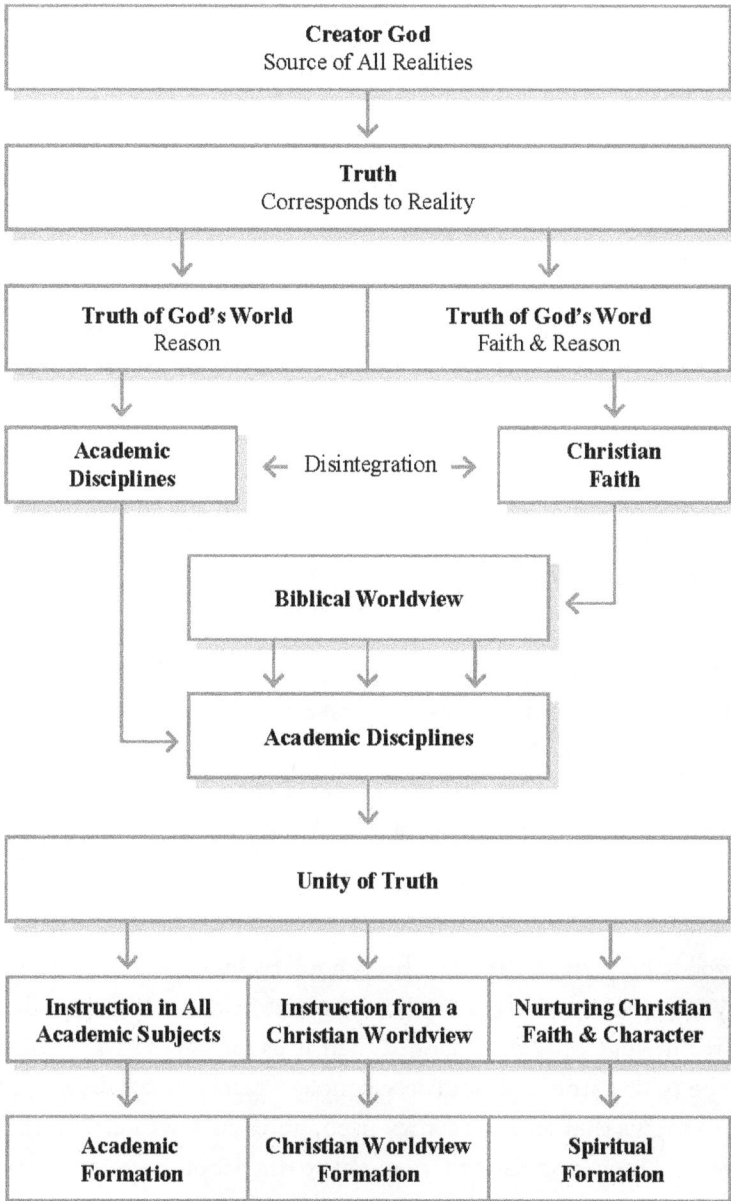

The Threefold Mission of Christian Schooling

In the next chapter we look at the role played by the school community and the faculty to accomplish all three aspects of the Christian-school mission.

8

The School Community and the Faculty

Impacting Students' Lives Forever

"The school community is not a passive place in which the Christian-school mission occurs, but an active, purposeful expression, even manifestation, of the shared values and unified vision of human flourishing central to the idea of a Christian school."

—TOM STONER

"If you send your children to this school, twenty years from now they will not be talking about how the turf field, new science lab, or 1:1 technology program changed their lives forever . . . Your child will be telling stories about these people—teachers, coaches, and the like—things they said, how they lived, notes they wrote, who they were, and how God used them to shape the people they are today."

—TOM STONER

Each time I speak to prospective parents considering enrolling their child in a Christian school, I tell them that two of the most valuable things we offer them and their children are the opportunity to be part of the school community and experience the influence of the faculty. Both aspects make vital contributions to the life-shaping mission of Christian schooling in students' lives.

THE ROLE OF THE SCHOOL COMMUNITY

The Christian-school community is equal parts delightful and powerful, for it has an educational force of its own. The school community is not a passive place in which the Christian-school mission occurs, but an active, purposeful expression, or even manifestation, of the shared values and unified vision of human flourishing central to the idea of a Christian school. The Christian-school mission enlivens the school community, and the school community facilitates the Christian-school mission. One author uses the term "functional communities"[78] to describe the active and mutually beneficial way the community contributes to the Christian-school mission.

Functional school communities provide students a place to belong and a convincing awareness that they are a part of something that is more than simply a collection of individuals. A community is a collection of individuals in a school, unified by a common vision for human flourishing and committed to the shared purpose of translating that vision to reality in the lives of everyone touched by it.[79]

This means that when the student body at a pep rally or the extended community at an all-school event shouts, "We are—COUGARS," their expression of school pride captures this sense of belonging; connection to the school creates strong attachments in ways similar to that of a family. When one member or group within the community achieves something or accomplishes a victory, the community celebrates, and the joy is multiplied. When one member or group within the community suffers disappointment or defeat, the community responds, and the negative impact is lessened.

This strong sense of connectedness rooted in a shared purpose and values creates something very valuable for students and treasured by parents: a type of positive peer pressure that influences students to think and act in ways consistent with the community's shared values of what is true, right, and good.[80] Imagine the power and value of a school community where students receive consistent encouragement from all school personnel, from other students—as well as parents whom they encounter in and out of school—to walk together against the prevailing winds of contemporary culture. Such a school community functions like a greenhouse for the cultivation of healthy friendships that are nurtured by an intentional program where students have fun and deepen relationships that in turn facilitate the school's mission.

Functional communities nourish the soul. All people who experience active and trusting connections to others cultivate characteristics that are good for society in general.[81] The converse is also true: the absence of a stable and cohesive social community can hinder children's moral and emotional development and even their cognitive growth toward rational autonomy.[82] Schools with a unified center of values rooted in a shared vision of human flourishing have even demonstrated reduced drop-out rates and other tangible benefits to students, including a reduction in the academic achievement gap.[83]

Parents find a valuable ally in a functional school community with shared commitments to a clear set of values at a time when economic realities and the rise of social media make parenting more complex and challenging than ever. A cohesive school community can help parents know what their children are doing as they get to know and become allies with the parents of their children's friends. When problems arise and it is necessary to contact the school or another parent in the community to resolve the sometimes messy issues of life, the alliance with the school and between families and accompanying spirit of "we are in this together" make it easier to work toward a common goal. Every member of the Christian-school community—students, parents, and all school personnel—is responsible to preserve and promote the distinctive school community; most schools ask each of them to sign an expression of their commitment to do so on an annual "Parent Agreement" or a statement of the school's shared values on a "Community Life Statement."

COMMUNITY AND THE THREEFOLD MISSION

The distinctive nature of the Christian-school community contributes to each aspect of the threefold mission of Christian schooling.

Regarding the academic mission, I recall a parent of students in a Christian school saying that when he transferred to the same Christian school (decades earlier), he noticed that his new friends there were serious about doing well in school, to prepare for a good college and a profession.

This changed his own attitude and altered the trajectory of his own academic aspirations. He credits the influence of classmates.

Second, we've discussed the integration of instruction in the classroom as the defining characteristic of the Christian-school mission and the highest priority for cultivating students' Christian worldviews. However, students also wrestle with the challenging issues of life more informally, with teachers after class, with coaches at practice, and directors at rehearsal breaks. Students engage in conversation with friends' parents when they are hanging out in homes, and with each other at innumerable times and in many venues in daily life together as they seek real answers to life's questions.

Finally, the context of a functional school community contributes to the mission of spiritual formation by serving as an extension of God's grace, love, and acceptance.

A DOSE OF REALITY

Christian school communities are far from perfect. When communicating with prospective parents, I find it important to check their expectations appropriately lest they be disillusioned the first time their child comes home with stories of the bad language, unkind words, and inappropriate behaviors that fall way short of Christian ideals. Christian schools deal with the same problems and realities that kids deal with in public and other private schools: alcohol, drugs, sex, depression, pride, and all the drama and relationship struggles faced by adolescents everywhere. The children in Christian schools were born with natural inclinations to think and act badly, a direct result of the original sin in the garden of Eden. Some students have come to a saving faith in Jesus Christ resulting in conversion and the presence of the Holy Spirit in their hearts. Many, however, have not, and even those who have done so are young in faith. All students are weak and imperfect, just like their parents, teachers, coaches, and others. What is more, we all live in a desperately broken world that markets its depravity and worldview of secularism to make both appear normal. Why then are we surprised when children who do not yet have faith or are very young in faith, who have imperfect parents, and who live in a fallen world, reflect these realities in their daily lives within our school?

The distinctive value and mission of the school community is defined less in terms of the sinful attitudes, thoughts, words, and actions that are somehow barred from entry and therefore absent within our walls. Would that we were better able to create schools that are the glass-bubbled shelters that some, especially critics, imagine them to be. Rather, the distinctive value of the Christian-school community is defined by what is present there: namely, a unified vision of what is required for our students to be all they are capable of being, rooted in the convictions of the historic Christian faith that gives rise to a set of beliefs and values shared by the extended community. Students' lives are shaped by encountering a consistent and pervasive presence of people walking in a specific direction while inviting, encouraging, teaching, disciplining, and imploring students to walk the same path with them.

THE POWER OF THE CHRISTIAN SCHOOL COMMUNITY IN TRAGEDY

Before school started one morning, my assistant handed me two messages from the father of a current student urging me to call him immediately. When I did, he informed me that his son, a sophomore just weeks away from getting his driver's license—a truly extraordinary young man in faith, character, and achievement in every arena—had gone to sleep early not feeling well and died inexplicably in his sleep.

What transpired in our school community in the hours, days, and weeks following the news of this tragedy was a visible, even tangible, manifestation of God's grace from the outpouring of grief, the shared suffering, and the collective expression of faith, hope, and love expressed among teachers, students, parents, and the broader school, church, and local community. The response of the community of faith in tragedy is the clearest witness to the reality of God in whom we believe and the truth for which our schools exist. The power of the community so clearly witnessed in times of tragedy is also the daily context supporting and advancing the life-shaping mission of Christian schooling. For all these reasons, we conclude with Vryhof: "the profoundly religious context of faith-based schooling should be of great interest to parents . . . who struggle with the question of how to pass on to their children their most deeply held beliefs and values."[84]

AN ENCOURAGING STUDY FOR ALL CHRISTIAN PARENTS

As a bridge to the role of the school faculty, I mention a study that highlights the mission of Christian schooling in general and the value of the school community specifically. Stephen Garber discovered that a shockingly high percentage of students aged eighteen to twenty-two raised in Christian homes walked away from Christian faith. His research focused upon the small percentage who remained in an effort to identify common characteristics that may have contributed to their faithfulness. His conclusions are revealing for our study on Christian schooling. Garber identified three factors woven throughout the life stories of those who remained faithful. During the critical years between adolescence and adulthood, the students who flourished in their lives (1) formed a worldview that answered life's questions, providing a coherent view of truth in a culture increasingly marked by secularization and pluralization; (2) met a teacher who modeled or incarnated the worldview they were in the process of assimilating into their own minds and hearts; and (3) forged friendships with others and made connection to a community whose common life offered a context for their shared values and convictions to be lived.[85] The mission of Christian schools incorporates all three factors: (1) the importance of worldview formation, (2) the impact of teachers, coaches, directors and all school personnel modeling Christian faith, worldview, and character in relationship with students, and (3) the power of the relationships in the daily life of the school community as an extension of the mission.

THE ROLE OF THE FACULTY

If the members of the extended school community are the supporting cast of the Christian-school mission, the members of the faculty—the teachers, coaches, performing arts directors, counselors, chaplains, and all the school personnel whose daily work finds them directly engaged with students— play the leading roles. When speaking to prospective parents contemplating sending their child to a Christian school, I often put up a picture of the faculty and say: "If you send your children to this school, twenty years from now they will not be talking about how the beautiful turf field or the new science lab or the 1:1 technology program changed their lives forever. These valuable things support and facilitate our mission. Your child will be telling stories about these people—teachers, coaches, and the like—things they said, how they lived, notes they wrote, who they were, and how God used them to shape the people they are today."

What makes me say this with such confidence? Some of the impact simply reflects the power of the teacher-student relationship. Jesus affirmed this power when he said, "A student is not above his teacher, but everyone who is fully trained will be like his teacher" (Luke 6:40). At my father's eightieth birthday party, I was amazed to hear him recite word for word the comment his fourth-grade teacher wrote in his yearbook seventy years earlier! Teachers everywhere, and in every type of school, have an extraordinary impact upon students' lives. Chances are good, as you think about the people who contributed to the person you are today, the name of a teacher, coach, or director from school comes to your mind.

I believe, however, that the impact of Christian-school teachers in the lives of students is increased and expanded in direct correlation to the ways the mission of Christian schooling is different from public and other private schools. It is the teachers' shared faith and commitment to the mission of Christian schooling that motivates them to give the best of who they are and what they do to fulfill the mission in the lives of the students. Research consistently captures this reality. Faculty in distinctive schools have a greater sense of shared mission and higher levels of job satisfaction despite the fact that their compensation levels consistently fall below those of public-school teachers.[86]

Students notice and remember the kindness of the faculty. In the middle of a school year, one grandparent told me that her elementary-aged grandson had said, "Grandma, my teacher loves me. I mean she really loves me." One researcher in Christian schooling observed what he described as "an infectious affection between teachers and students that made education effective and meaningful."[87] The faculty is the embodiment of the Christian-school mission, the "living curriculum," who together make the threefold mission of Christian schooling a reality in daily practice.

THE FACULTY AND THE THREEFOLD MISSION OF CHRISTIAN SCHOOLING

Teachers build students' *academic foundations*. Great teachers teach with a passion for the academic content that is infectious and makes the students love the content the way they do. I'll never forget listening to an English professor lecturing on a novel. His passion for the material caused him to become emotional to such a degree that through tears he said, "Class dismissed!" and walked out of the classroom. I probably snickered along with many other students at the abbreviated class, but thirty years later I'm writing about it. A teacher's love for the academic material and a coach's love for the best practices of her sport is born of her own study, is reinforced by her daily preparation, and is expressed by high expectations and an attitude that echoes, "This stuff is important for it is God's truth we are dealing with!" Teachers celebrate hard work, individual progress, and achievement while casting a vision for how students' academic preparation and reaching their full potential are essential to finding their calling and flourishing throughout their lives.

Teachers shape students' *Christian worldview*. In his groundbreaking book *The Pattern of Truth*, Frank Gaebelein recounts a conversation he had with C. S. Lewis in his office at Oxford University, in which they affirmed the inescapable fact: "the worldview of the teacher . . . gradually conditions the worldview of the pupil."[88] Indeed, the faculty, coaches, and directors translate the idea of a Christian worldview into a living and breathing reality in their instruction and by their example. Teachers shape students' minds and hearts as they wrestle with the academic content through the lens of a Christian worldview in class and as the conversations spill over into the hallways, at school events, and anytime teachers engage with students. This powerful reality over time, as all faculty and students experience daily life together, imparts to students the shared vision of human flourishing that defines Christian schooling.

Finally, God uses teachers, coaches, directors, and all school personnel as instruments of students' *spiritual formation* as these staff members share their journey to faith and invite students to walk the path of discipleship with them to become the people God created them to be. The essential priority is to hire Christian teachers who have experienced God's grace and who in turn are able to cultivate a classroom, team, cast, or community where the relationships between teacher and students—and students with other students—are characterized by the gracious affirmation of each person's intrinsic worth from being created by God and made in his image. To dispense grace, teachers—and all school personnel—must understand what it is and its fundamental opposition to the toxic spirit of legalism, where a teacher's favor is given or withheld based upon the student's performance.

All school personnel embody grace by sending inviting messages: "I like what you did"; "I'm glad you are part of this team"; and "We missed you."[89] The most powerful times for such messages are when students get a low grade, drop a winning pass, or get in trouble. The words "I'm still with you"; "we all learn through mistakes"; and "we'll get through this" can change a student's life forever.

The idea of a Christian school combined with a dedicated faculty motivated to make its unified vision of human flourishing a reality in the lives of every student results in a life-shaping educational experience told by students in stories of how their teachers, coaches, and directors contributed to helping them become the people they are today. Our own daughter, when in the fifth grade, had such an outstanding teacher that at the end of the year she declared, "I want to be just like her." Today she is teaching fourth grade in a Christian school—just like that teacher! One Thanksgiving, we loved hosting a former student, then studying music performance at a college in our region. As we each expressed something for which we were grateful to God, he named his elementary and middle-school music teacher for inspiring him to pursue his passion for music and giving him a vision for being the man God created him to be. Multiply these stories by millions of Christian-school alumni around the world, and we begin to see the global impact of the worldwide mission of Christian schooling.

A PERSONAL EXAMPLE

In a file in my desk I keep a note from Dr. Gerry Hawthorne, my Greek professor at Wheaton College. For two semesters of New Testament Greek, he inspired me and so many others to give our best to our studies. Always prepared for class, he made us love Greek the way he did.

After these two semesters, the only way for me to continue with Professor Hawthorne was to take a semester of Classical Greek, translating Plato's *Apology*. I was drowning in the challenging material combined with the inevitable personal challenges of college life. As I gasped for air in the class, I received back a quiz I had taken on which I had done poorly. As I went over all the red ink on the papers, I noticed that he had altered some of my answers and changed the grade at the top of the first page using white out, because he couldn't bear to give me the grade I actually deserved. On the last page of the quiz I found this note:

Tom, you are going down instead of up. I'm failing you [letting you down]! What can I do to help remedy this slide you are in? You've the potential for the best and if you are going to be a leader in the church, right here—mastering Greek, is the place to start. I'd love to be in on this venture. In love, gfh

There are many things that contributed to the power of this note. The first is that he was my biggest advocate and was so committed to me that he took responsibility for my poor performance saying, "I'm failing you!" Also, his note came at a time when I was struggling, which made its impact far greater than if I had been hitting it out of the park. Such a note at a time of struggle short-circuited the performance-based-acceptance wiring in my mind and heart, allowing God's grace to penetrate very deeply. Professor Hawthorne also cast a vision for my life that looked far beyond my current circumstances. Where did he get the idea that I might be a leader in the church? With what eyes was he seeing? In doing so, he also highlighted the essential value of academic preparation for the future saying, "Right here— mastering Greek, is the place to start." Finally, he expressed the depth of his commitment to me by saying he'd "love to be in on this venture," and he signed it, "in love," using the Greek word *agape*, used to describe the unconditional love that God has for his people.

This note, written on the back of a weekly quiz by a Christian-school teacher, still touches a deep part of my heart thirty years after it was written. Its brief message captures all the elements of the mission of Christian schooling brought to life through the role of the teacher, resulting in a life changed forever. These notes flow freely from the pens of Christian-school teachers around the world.

```
┌─────────────────────────────────────────────────┐
│                  Creator God                     │
│              Source of All Realities             │
└─────────────────────────────────────────────────┘
                        ↓
┌─────────────────────────────────────────────────┐
│                     Truth                        │
│              Corresponds to Reality              │
└─────────────────────────────────────────────────┘
          ↓                            ↓
┌────────────────────────┬────────────────────────┐
│   Truth of God's World │   Truth of God's Word   │
│        Reason          │      Faith & Reason     │
└────────────────────────┴────────────────────────┘
          ↓                            ↓
┌──────────────────┐              ┌──────────────────┐
│    Academic      │ ← Disintegration →│   Christian   │
│   Disciplines    │              │      Faith        │
└──────────────────┘              └──────────────────┘
                  ┌─────────────────────────┐   ↓
                  │    Biblical Worldview    │ ←
                  └─────────────────────────┘
                     ↓        ↓        ↓
        →  ┌─────────────────────────────┐
           │     Academic Disciplines     │
           └─────────────────────────────┘
                        ↓
┌─────────────────────────────────────────────────┐
│                 Unity of Truth                   │
└─────────────────────────────────────────────────┘
      ↓                 ↓                 ↓
┌─────────────────────────────────────────────────┐
│             Christian School Mission             │
├──────────────┬──────────────┬──────────────────┤
│  Academic    │  Worldview    │    Spiritual     │
│  Formation   │  Formation    │    Formation     │
├──────────────┴──────────────┴──────────────────┤
│       Role of School Community & Faculty         │
└─────────────────────────────────────────────────┘
```

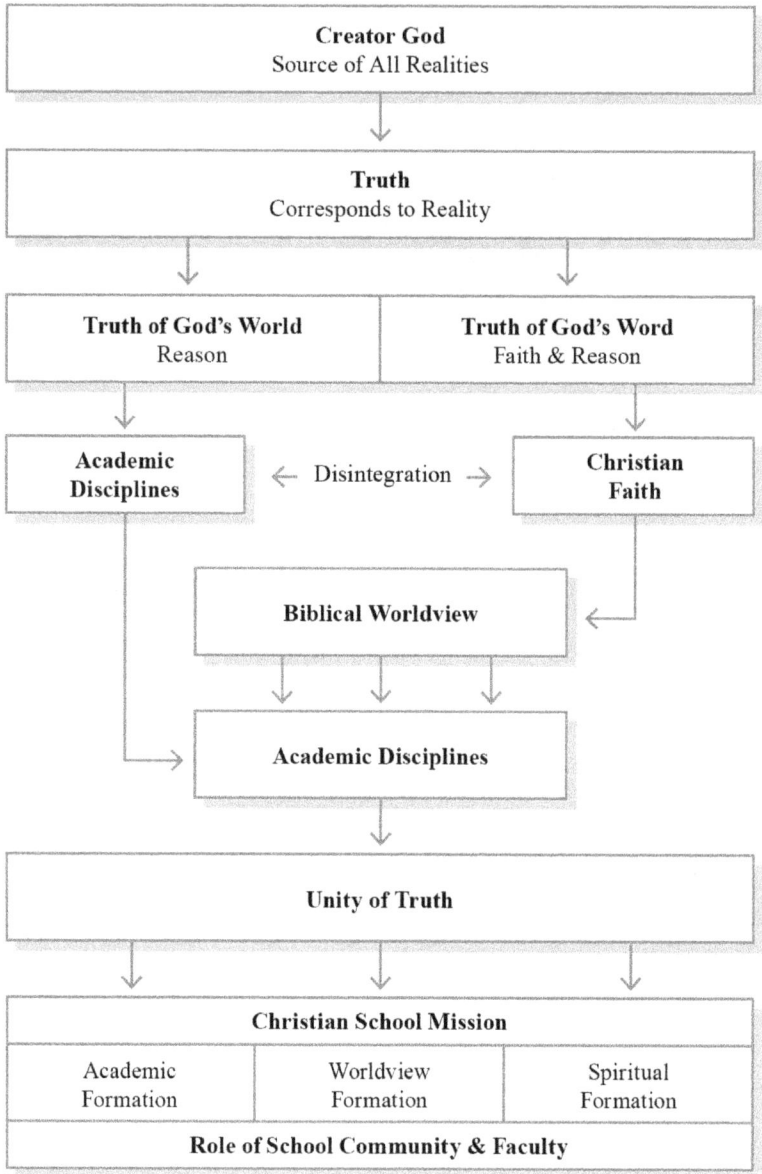

The Essential Role of the Community and Faculty

CHAPTER SUMMARY

The school community is an active, purposeful part of the Christian-school mission that influences students' lives for good by creating connections for students and presenting them with a visible expression of the shared vision of human flourishing through relationships with other students, all faculty and staff, and other parents. The school community is far from perfect but contributes to all three aspects of the Christian-school mission: academic, worldview, and spiritual formation. It can be particularly powerful in the face of life's tragedies as it embodies the grace, truth, and shared vision of life essential to helping students flourish despite the deepening influences present in culture today.

The single greatest influence in the lives of Christian-school students is from the faculty. The role of teachers, coaches, and directors is powerful in any school context but their influence is heightened in direct correlation to the elements that define the Christian-school mission. The faculty help students grasp the importance of understanding God's truth in the academic curriculum as preparation for their futures. They also provide a living picture of the Christian worldview as they help cultivate students' worldviews in and out of the classroom. Finally, they model lives changed by the grace and truth of Jesus Christ. In these ways the faculty and staff embody the Christian-school mission and serve as instruments God uses to impact students forever.

Each element of the idea of a Christian school considered to this point is an essential piece, a building block, preparing us to reach our current point where we reflect on the ultimate goal of Christian schooling. We turn to this now in the final chapter.

9

Bringing It All Together

*The Goal of Christian Schooling
and Helping Children Flourish*

"A Christian in any occupation seeks to do the job in a way that expands the kingdom of God on earth by reflecting truth, beauty, love, justice, and all the attributes of God's character."
—TOM STONER

"The place God calls you to is the place where your deep gladness and the world's deep hunger meet."
—FREDERICK BUECHNER

This chapter asks the fundamental question, what is the goal of Christian schooling? In other words, if Christian schools accomplish their distinctive mission, what will be the outcome in students' lives? What return on the investment of time, tuition, and financial gifts might grandparents, parents, and students expect? What will students ultimately be prepared to do? How will they live in a way that causes them to flourish and be all that God created them to be? To provide a complete answer, we need to briefly review the essential elements of the Christian-school mission.

THE GOAL OF THE CHRISTIAN-SCHOOL MISSION AND PREPARING CHILDREN TO FLOURISH

Each of the elements described in the previous chapters contribute to the Christian-school mission and helps prepare students to flourish in their lives and become the people God created them to be. But what does it look like to bring these elements together in an all-encompassing vision for human flourishing? Or to ask it another way: "What will it look like for the students in our schools to flourish in their lives?"

In the same way that the defining mark of a Christian-school education is the integration of the truth of the historic Christian faith with academic learning, an integrated vision of the goal of Christian schooling defines student flourishing in terms of preparation for academic and cultural engagement—finding what God has called them to do, and doing it in a way that expands the kingdom of God by adding truth, beauty, love, and justice in the world.

Preparation for academic and cultural engagement is not a distraction to the Christian-school mission but an indispensable and central part of it. Frank Gaebelein believed that scholarship and leadership are synonymous. The call to intellectual scholarship is rooted in the fact that education is always shaped by a vision of what is required for human flourishing, which is sometimes characterized by the biblical word *shalom*. Therefore, when Christian schools prepare students to engage the culture as witnesses to the full breadth of God's truth in creation, in the Scriptures, and in Christ, we not only prepare our students to flourish as individuals but also to lead others toward truth and human flourishing. The Christian-school mission to impact culture in this way requires the cultivation of our students' minds as well as their hearts and a call to Christian scholarship that is facilitated by the deliberate cultivation of students' Christian worldviews and supported by authentic Christian faith and character. This is precisely the rallying cry of Robert Harris, who says the world needs

> deeply learned and fully integrated Christian philosophers, intellectuals, scientists, historians, novelists, journalists, good thinkers of every kind. Ideas are fought with ideas. If no one brings to bear the powerful thinking needed to combat error, then error will lie back, grow fat, and rule the world. We need Christians who can outthink the secularists (the philosophical naturalists and the postmodernists). There are many gaping holes in their worldviews

and in their methodologies, and we need Christians to drive a truck though those holes, honking the horn.[90]

We want to prepare our graduates to be leaders in every academic field, in athletics, and in the arts. They will be called to careers in law, business, medicine, education, engineering, politics, the trades, and all types of social services. While they fulfill these callings, they will be active participants in the worldwide mission of the Christian church, working to strengthen their families, and serving in their local churches and communities. As they live and work in all these areas, we see them advancing new ideas, addressing injustices, contributing to best practices, and engaging every discussion with ideas reflecting a Christian worldview that is rooted in a unified, cohesive, and complete understanding of truth corresponding to all the created realities of the world around them. This is the first element of human flourishing and the first goal of an integrated vision of Christian schooling.

The second resists the duality that views full-time Christian service as separate from *secular life* in favor of a perspective that integrates work with Christian mission. This integrated perspective views the purpose of Christian schooling not only to prepare students to participate in the fulfillment of the Great Commission given by Jesus to make disciples of all nations, but also to prepare them to participate in the fulfillment of the *cultural mandate* given by God to Adam and Eve in Genesis 1:26, 28:

> Then God said, "Let us make mankind in our image, in our likeness, so that they may rule over the fish in the sea and the birds in the sky, over the livestock and all the wild animals, and over all the creatures that move along the ground." . . . God blessed them and said to them, "Be fruitful and increase in number; fill the earth and subdue it. Rule over the fish in the sea and the birds in the sky and over every living creature that moves on the ground."

Fulfilling the cultural mandate is part of what it means to be human—created in the image of God. The way students learn to "rule over creation" is by discovering just what it is they are called to do—the specific vocation for which they have a passion and are uniquely gifted, and where they are able to simultaneously work as contributing members of society and as members of the kingdom of God. "Each of us must find an occupation so intrinsically valuable and so naturally suited to us that, through it, we may add to the treasure of the kingdom."[91] In finding this place to use their particular interests, gifts, and talents, our students will find deep, joyful, and meaningful fulfillment. They will be fully alive themselves and help others become fully alive at the same time. This place of deep fulfillment and impact on others is captured in Frederick Buechner's definition of calling: "The place God calls you to is the place where your deep gladness and the world's deep hunger meet."[92]

Students will flourish in their lives and feel fully alive by finding what it is that God has created, gifted, and called them to do. In this place they will build relationships with colleagues, customers, vendors, and others with whom they will have the opportunity to be witnesses to the truth of the gospel of Jesus Christ, leading to others becoming his disciples. In this place they will also fulfill the cultural mandate by creating or accomplishing a job that uses their God-given skills and abilities to reason, create, harvest, or employ the resources of creation to make a living and care for the needs of their families in a way that also contributes to the common betterment and good. The second element of an integrated philosophy of the goal of Christian schooling is graduating students with a vision to find their vocational calling—what it is that God has uniquely created and gifted them to do.

The third goal of an integrated philosophy of Christian schooling is preparing students to graduate with a vision not only to find *what* God has called them to do but also *how* God intends for them to do it. Students will flourish in their lives by fulfilling their calling in a way that adds truth, beauty, love, and justice to a world that desperately needs it. This is what it means to engage culture by being an instrument of the restoration and redemption made possible through the life, death, and resurrection of Jesus Christ. In the words of Cornelius Plantinga:

> [W]e must not only find an occupation to bring to the kingdom; we must *shape* it to suit this purpose. The point is that occupations are often valuable to the kingdom, but only if we reform them. So in today's world, perhaps a Christian would shape the occupation of quality-control supervisor by encouraging whistle-blowers instead of retaliating against them. Perhaps a Christian would shape the occupation of computer repair technician by doing top-notch diagnoses in order to save customers the expense of unnecessary repairs. Perhaps a Christian would shape the occupation of CEO of a major airline by telling its customers the truth about flight cancellations and delays. In any case, occupational reforms serve the kingdom of God as surely as a Billy Graham Crusade does.[93]

A Christian in any occupation seeks to do the job in a way that expands the kingdom of God on earth by reflecting truth, beauty, love, justice, and all the attributes of God's character.

As I write this, I cannot help but think about a young woman who scooped ice cream at a small shop in a Christian community near Lake Michigan where my parents have a summer cottage. I quickly noticed how intentionally she worked, greeting customers warmly, completing their orders efficiently, serving portions toward the generous end of what is appropriate, and supporting coworkers by ensuring supplies were fully stocked. An employer would rarely envision such an ideal worker whose motivation for such excellence was intrinsic to the young woman and an outworking of her faith and character.

For students, Christian-worldview living need not wait until they are employed in the area of their vocational calling but can begin the moment they understand that God is honored both by what they do and how they do it. They can reflect this as students by being on time for class, doing their best work, listening when appropriate, contributing where possible, and being respectful of the teacher and fellow students at all times.

A REAL-LIFE EXAMPLE

A clear example of the threefold mission of Christian schooling and illustration of its goal is a friend who attended a Christian school as a boy. He then majored in economics at Wheaton College. After graduation, he entered the field of international banking. Early in his career, he worked in a newly developing complex segment of the industry known as derivatives, which companies and investors use to manage their debt and offset risks from market volatility. Because derivative transactions involve very small margins or interest rate changes, they generally involve big sums of money and high risk.

As my friend observed more and more derivative transitions, he realized that many users of these products were at a serious disadvantage because the selling financial institution nearly always had the advantage of more market information. This made the transactions patently unfair. My friend heard the negative stories from purchasers being exploited and saw how the imbalance of information contributed to a growing trust gap between people on Main Street and the financial institutions on Wall Street. Instead of using his company's knowledge and experience to profit from this unjust imbalance of information, he founded a company intent on providing buyers with transparent information about market pricing and his own company's pricing. His company prioritized trust rather than profit, which created tremendous loyalty with clients. Driven by loyalty and trust, his company has grown over decades to hundreds of employees now serving clients in offices around the world. In a market culture where trust is scarce, his company has demonstrated there is another way to do business.

The story of my friend and his company illustrates each element of the threefold mission of Christian schooling. The company's ability to serve clients required him and his colleagues to be excellent bankers, prepared with the knowledge and understanding of math, finance, banking, business, economics, as well as the skills to think, analyze, synthesize, create, communicate, and more—all of which are cultivated over time, year after year, as part of the academic formation that takes place in school. The company was founded because he identified a perceived injustice and set out to make it right by creating transparency in derivative financial transactions. The company's vision to be an agent of restoration in the financial industry is a great example of viewing a vocation through the lens of a Christian worldview. Finally, the enduring motivation that prioritizes trust above bottom-line profits, while intentionally cultivating redemptive relationships with a growing number of people, reflects the change of heart and mind resulting from authentic spiritual formation.

CHRISTIAN SCHOOLING AND THE GLORY OF THE LIVING GOD

The earliest memory I have of my life-shaping years in a Christian school was arriving in the summer for the first day of soccer preseason training camp. It was August 1981, and I was fourteen years old. After gathering by the parking lot, the coach walked us toward the field and then asked us to sit under a tree for some opening remarks on our season. For many of the freshmen, the meeting was the start of our Christian-school experience. I can picture the scene: my coach flipping pages in his Bible before reading from 1 Corinthians 10:31, "So, whether you eat or drink or whatever you do, do it all for the glory of God." He challenged us to play soccer that season in a way that brings glory to God. In so doing, my freshman soccer coach planted the idea in our minds, from the truth of God's Word, that

God has designed us in such a way that everything we do can be done for the glory of the living God.

Turning our attention to the glory of the living God is a fitting end to *The Idea of a Christian School*, for we began with parents' deeply held right to choose the nature of their child's schooling rooted in the long-standing tradition in education that the cultivation of the mind is inextricably bound to the cultivation of the heart and character. Real education, therefore, pursues a vision of what is required for students to flourish in their lives and be all they are capable of being. The Christian school is founded upon the belief that there is a true and living God, the creator of all things in heaven and on earth, who has revealed himself in the world he has made and in his Word—Jesus Christ the living Word, and the written words of Scripture. At a time when all of society, and especially public schools and private schools that are not intentionally religious, sharply dis-integrate the study of truth discovered in creation through the academic disciplines from the truth of the historic Christian faith, the Christian school integrates these dimensions of truth to provide students with a complete, cohesive, and unified understanding of the world. Through its threefold mission of academic formation, Christian worldview formation, and spiritual formation, the Christian school prepares students to engage culture and to flourish in their lives by finding their individual calling—the place of their passion and giftedness. From this place they will fulfill the cultural mandate by working to reshape the creation as instruments of the restoration Jesus Christ came to bring. From this place they will also participate in the Great Commission to make disciples of all nations, reconciling people to God through the relationships they establish with family, friends, colleagues, and others they encounter in their daily lives.

Each of these elements of the Christian-school mission combine together to create a clear picture of what it means for humans to flourish and be all they are capable of being. Now we end by considering the highest expression of human flourishing and the ultimate purpose for which we were created: *the glory of the living God.* This truth is captured in the historic creeds and confessions of the Christian faith, though none more clearly than the first question of the Westminster Shorter Catechism, which answers the question of the "chief end" or ultimate purpose of humankind this way: "to glorify God and to enjoy him forever."[94] But what exactly is the glory of God? And how does the goal of Christian schooling help students to live in a way that increases God's glory?

WHAT IS THE GLORY OF GOD?

The Bible describes the glory of God in several important ways. In Psalm 19, David writes: "The heavens declare the glory of God; the skies proclaim the work of his hands." We see God's glory in the creation God made; its beauty and complexity reflect the fingerprints of its maker. Similarly, Jesus's beloved disciple, John, writes these unforgettable words in the opening verses of his Gospel: "The Word became flesh and made his dwelling among us. We have seen his glory, the glory of the one and only Son, who came from the Father, full of grace and truth" (John 1:14). Jesus Christ, God made flesh, is the perfect representation of the glory of God in a human person.

Finally, Moses asked God directly: "Show me your glory." Amazingly, God complied with Moses's request and said: "I will cause all my *goodness* to pass in front of you, and I will *proclaim my name*, the Lord, in your presence." Then God hid Moses in the cleft of a rock and allowed his presence to pass by so that Moses saw a glimpse of his back, for God said, "[Y]ou cannot see my face, for no one may see me and live" (Exodus 33:18–20, italics added). Throughout the pages of Scripture, the glory of God is synonymous with his name and the reality of who he is: the work of his hands in creation and history, the Word made flesh in the person of Jesus Christ, and all the qualities attributed to his perfect character.

So what does it look like for us, our children, and the students in our schools, to live in a way that gives God glory? We bring glory to God when we look at the world God made—the heavens and the earth, whether in the study of an academic subject or everyday life, and catch a glimpse of something inspiring awe and wonder, and say: "Wow! Look at that. God made it! Isn't he good?" We also bring glory to God when we, creatures made by the creator God, fashioned in his image and likeness, accomplish something noteworthy, act skillfully, create beauty, or do anything in a way that is excellent or praiseworthy, pause to acknowledge God as the source of our lives and talents. In these ways we join with the psalmist David in saying: "Ascribe to the Lord the glory due his name" (Psalm 29:2).

We also bring glory to God as our minds are renewed to think godly thoughts and the affections of our hearts are changed to love God and others, so that we become the people he intended us to be and reflect in increasing measure his image—the image of Jesus Christ—by the work of his Spirit in our hearts. The apostle Paul describes the way the transformation of our lives reflects his glory this way: "And we all, who with unveiled faces contemplate the Lord's glory, are being transformed into his image with ever-increasing glory, which comes from the Lord, who is the Spirit" (2 Corinthians 3:18). We reflect God's glory in our lives as our hearts are changed—truth replacing error, love replacing harm, and we are restored as individual persons to reflect the image God intended for us at creation.

Finally, we bring God glory as instruments God uses to restore creation by identifying our calling and doing our work in a way that adds truth, beauty, justice and love—and all the virtues of the God who made us—in our lost and broken world.

In so doing, we become fully alive and experience the deepest satisfaction of our hearts, souls, minds, and strength as we contribute to the expansion of the kingdom that will have no end and fulfill the purpose for which we were made.

> Praise be to the LORD GOD, the God of Israel,
> who alone does marvelous deeds.
> Blessed be to his glorious name forever;
> may the whole earth be filled with his glory.
> Amen and Amen. (Psalm 72:18–19)

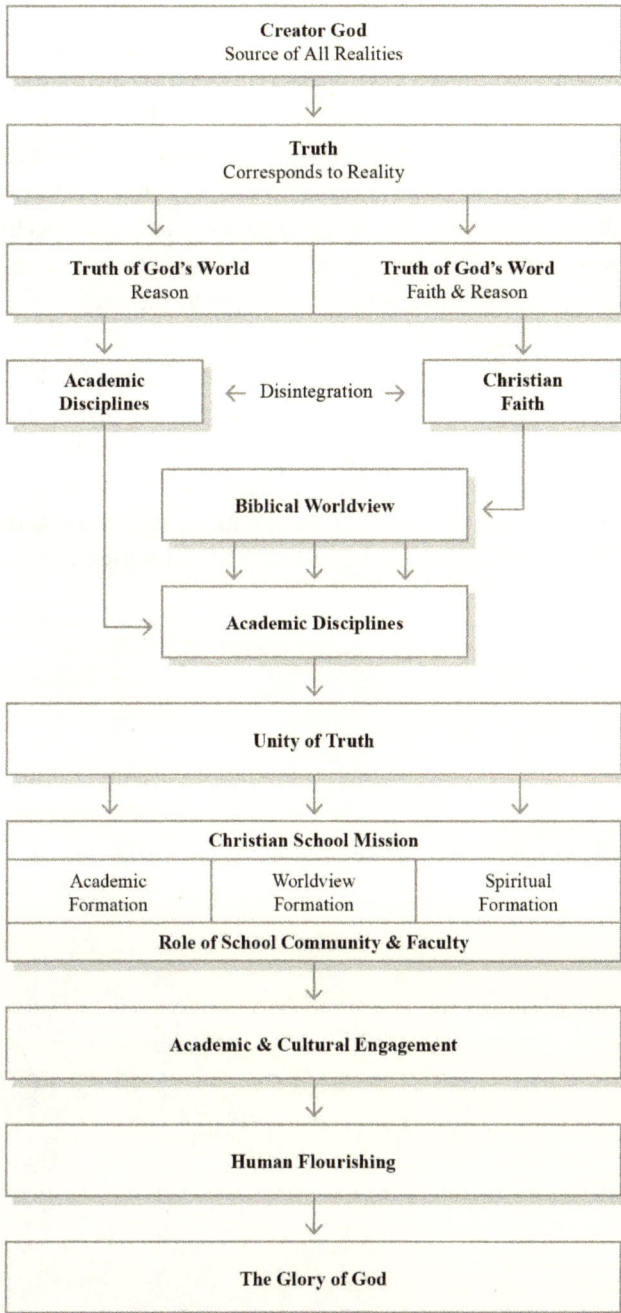

Creator God
Source of All Realities

Truth
Corresponds to Reality

Truth of God's World
Reason

Truth of God's Word
Faith & Reason

**Academic
Disciplines**

← Disintegration →

**Christian
Faith**

Biblical Worldview

Academic Disciplines

Unity of Truth

Christian School Mission

Academic Formation	Worldview Formation	Spiritual Formation

Role of School Community & Faculty

Academic & Cultural Engagement

Human Flourishing

The Glory of God

A Summary of the Idea of a Christian School

CHAPTER SUMMARY

This chapter answers the question toward which each previous chapter provides an essential building block: "What is the goal of Christian schooling?" The answer is simply to prepare students to engage the academic disciplines and all of culture as instruments of truth and justice, and as agents of the restoration Jesus Christ came to bring. In this way, they will be prepared to identify the area of their calling to any and every field and vocation and to live in a way that fulfills both the cultural mandate to "rule over creation" and the Great Commission to take the gospel to the ends of the earth. In doing so they will discover not only what they are called to do, but also how they are called to do it as agents of the kingdom of God. The goal of Christian schooling is to prepare students to be fully alive and to live in a way that brings glory to the living God by identifying the majesty of God's character in creation, by reflecting God's glory in their individual lives through growth into the image of Jesus Christ, and by expanding God's glory by living and working as instruments of restoration in this dark and broken world.

Endnotes

CHAPTER 1

1. Glenn, "Real Education," 41–50.
2. The literature on the value-laden nature of schooling is vast. In my study, I owe a debt to Stephen Vryhof, *Between Memory and Vision*.
3. Scholars Concerned About Advanced Placement History, "Letter Opposing APUSH Frameworks," 2015. .
4. Vryhof, *Between Memory and Vision*, 7.
5. National Center for Education Statistics (NCES), 2022.

CHAPTER 2

6. Another important text is the apostle Paul's writing to the Romans (1:20): "For since the creation of the world God's invisible qualities—his eternal power and divine nature—have been clearly seen, being understood from what has been made, so that people are without excuse."
7. These Scripture references in order are 2 Timothy 3:16; John 17:17, John 1:14; John 14:6.
8. The Belgic Confession of 1561, Article 2.
9. Gaebelein, *Pattern of God's Truth,* 1954. Gaebelein's book was first delivered as a series of lectures at Dallas Theological Seminary and later published by Oxford University Press. It is difficult to overstate the influence of this book; a major reason for its influence no doubt is that the ideas it expresses were forged on the anvil of actual practice in his work as the founding head of The Stony Brook School on Long Island, New York. This book more than any other set the trajectory for the movement of Christian schooling we see today.
10. Augustine, *On Christian Doctrine*, 2.18.28. If it would be difficult to overstate the contribution Gaebelein made to Christian schooling, it would be impossible to overstate the contribution Augustine made to all of Christian thought. The quotation attributed to Sir Isaac Newton: "If I have seen further, it is by standing on the shoulders of giants" captures well the contributions of thinkers such as Augustine whose ideas have shaped not just Christian schooling but our understanding of the truth of Christ as we know it.
11. Citation of Abraham Kuyper's inaugural address in 1880 at the dedication of the Free University of Amsterdam. Mark Noll expands this thought in his excellent book *Jesus*

Christ and the Life of the Mind, 25: "Put most simply, for believers to be studying created things is to be studying the works of Christ . . . There is simply nothing humanly possible to study about the created realm that, in principle, leads us away from Jesus Christ. To be sure, humans may misunderstand knowledge gained by studying the world, put it to evil uses, transform it into an idol, or otherwise abuse it. But these shortcomings do not alter the fact that, in the biblical view, the world was brought into existence by Jesus Christ."

12. Ron Chadwick rejects the distinction between sacred and secular truth but draws a distinction between truth revealed by God in the Bible and truth discovered in creation. Discovered truth he refers to as "mundane." Chadwick writes, "God is the source, the *quelle* of all truth that ever was, or is, or yet will be. A distinction still must be observed between revealed truth as declared by God and mundane truth as discovered by man, for man's relationship to his Creator is dependent upon the revelation of God in the Scriptures and not mundane or discovered truth," *Teaching and Learning*, 42. The distinction may be helpful to recognize that discovered truth may be more vulnerable to the distortions of human reason and understanding. The distinction is not helpful, however, to understanding the unified nature of truth.

13. Gaebelein, *Pattern of God's Truth*, 22.

14. Genesis 1:27 affirms that the capacities associated with the image of God are imparted to all people; James 3:9 affirms that these capacities extend to all beyond the fall. The fall of humankind influenced the inclinations of the human heart and resulted in the use of these capacities in ways very contrary to God's intention at creation, for evil rather than for good. Animals do not possess the same capacity to reason about the world.

15. Emphasis mine. The cultural mandate is an essential component of being created in the image of God. God has imparted to humans certain capacities that are necessary to fulfill the mandate by ruling over creation and subduing it. The cultural mandate was given before the fall as it was part of God's intention for his creation. Humans were created to use their God-given capacities and gifts to engage in meaningful work. After the fall, God initiates his plan by which creation will be redeemed and this plan culminates in Jesus issuing the Great Commission to make disciples of all nations (Matthew 28). All Christians are called by Christ to participate in the Great Commission as they also fulfill the cultural mandate by finding the place of their vocational calling.

16. Lewis, "Is Theology Poetry?," 17.

17. Some philosophers use the term *suprarational* to describe ideas that are neither rational nor irrational.

18. Newman, *Idea of a University*, 121.

19. These phrases are taken from Romans 1:21–22 and Ephesians 4:18.

20. For a helpful discussion of the relationship between faith and knowledge see Holmes, *All Truth Is God's Truth*, 73.

21. Here I also owe a debt to Spears and Loomis, *Education for Human Flourishing*. They write: "The combination of our rational capacities and the grace given to us through the revelation of God enables us to be educated. The symbiotic relationship between rationality and revelation enables us to craft the most complete view of reality," 43.

CHAPTER 3

22. Gaebelein "Toward a Philosophy of Christian Education," 37.

23. Harris, *Integration of Faith and Learning*, 24.

24. Gaebelein, *Pattern of God's Truth*, 31.

25. Gaebelein, *Pattern of God's Truth*, 31–34. The advancement Gaebelein is describing is radio-carbon dating. When he was writing, the field of science was limited in its ability to measure trace amounts of carbon, but the instruments of science were sufficient enough to date items in creation beyond six thousand years old. The traditional understanding of the age of the earth in Gaebelein's day was six thousand, which was not derived through the study of science, but by adding up the genealogies mentioned in the Bible. One of my Old Testament professors in seminary taught us the genealogies of the Bible are not complete but selective. The biblical authors may have left out dozens or hundreds of names in between the names they selected to include in the biblical genealogies. Given this misunderstanding of the genealogies and the subsequent misinterpretation of the age of the earth, there is a strong parallel to Copernican astronomy. The intention of the genealogies of the Bible is not to tell us when creation happened, in the same way the psalm is not intending to tell us how the planets are positioned in relation to the sun. The field of science contributes data to help us understand how old the earth is and how the planets move and the Bible reveals who God is and his plan of redemption. At the heart is how the data of science relate to the content of the Bible and how to properly interpret them both.

26. Cited in Kienel, "Philosophy of Christian School Education," iv.

27. Parsons, *Inside America's Christian Schools*, x.

28. Kienel, "Philosophy of Christian School Education," iv.

29. During my doctoral research, I found a number of humorous attempts at finding data from the academic disciplines in the pages of Scripture. When asked to describe how the Bible related to the academic content, one math teacher responded in a survey that he had heard one Old Testament passage contained a calculation "roughly equivalent to pi" (the common mathematical calculation for the circumference of a circle). I say "humorous," because I would imagine that if God had intended to provide this calculation in the Bible he would have gotten it right. Regarding this effort to find content in the Bible related to the academic disciplines, I mention the work of Ruth Haycock, whose *Encyclopedia of Bible Truths* (Colorado Springs: ACSI, 1993) is organized by academic subjects and provides chapter and verse where a verse might relate to chemistry, writing, sex education, and zoology. No doubt this work is motivated by a desire to affirm the authority of the Bible in academic study, however, it reflects a fundamental misunderstanding of both the message of the Bible and the validity of the truth discovered in the study of creation through the academic disciplines.

30. Occasionally the relationship between Christian faith and academic study breaks through the surface and is thrust into the public square. One such example of this happened in 2006, when the University of California (UC) rejected upper-level high-school transfer credits from a particular group of Christian schools. The rejected credits were from thirty-eight courses in subjects ranging from science and history to literature and government, all having used textbooks by fundamentalist Christian publishers. The Association of Christian Schools International (ACSI) argued the case as *viewpoint discrimination* and thus a violation of the Free Speech Clause guaranteed by the First Amendment. The defense argued that it admits transfer credits only from courses it has approved, to ensure that "admitted students took courses that provided those students with the knowledge and skills to succeed in their studies at UC." One expert faculty witness in the UC Science Department argued in favor of the decision by the UC to reject the transfer credits, asserting that "By teaching students to reject scientific evidence and

methodology whenever they might be inconsistent with the Bible they fail to teach the critical analysis skills required for careful scientific analysis." In 2008, the court ruled in favor of UC, stating that ACSI had failed to establish that the basis for the university's decision to reject the transfer credits was the religious viewpoints of the textbooks. Rather, the basis was informed by concerns more routine to the practices of college admissions departments.

31. Smith, *Bible Made Impossible*, 89, speaks well to this crisis of faith created by what he calls "Biblicism" or a misguided understanding of the Bible. He writes: "Biblicism often paints smart, committed youth into a corner that is for real reasons impossible to occupy for many of those who actually confront its problems. When some of those youth give up on Biblicism and simply walk away across the wet paint, it is flawed Biblicism that is partly responsible for those losses of faith."

32. Augustine, cited in Mark Noll, *Jesus Christ and the Life of the Mind*, 100–101.

33. The Belgic Confession of 1561, Article 2.

34. Williamson, *Shorter Catechism* 1, 10.

35. J. I. Packer, "Bible in Use: Evangelicals Seeking Truth from Holy Scripture," cited in Noll, *Jesus Christ and the Life*, 127.

36. Holmes, *All Truth Is God's Truth*, uses the term "limits," while Graham, *Teaching Redemptively*, uses the term "boundaries" to describe the same idea.

37. Noll, *Jesus Christ and the Life*, 128.

38. Plantinga, *Engaging God's World*, 24.

39. The origin of this phrase is ambiguous. It is often attributed to Galileo but seems more accurately attributed to the Italian Cardinal Caesar Baronius.

40. Noll, *Jesus Christ and the Life*, 124.

CHAPTER 4

41. Various authors use these different terms. Gaebelein uses "grid"; Dilthey, "set of mental categories"; M. Eckel, *Whole Truth* "frame of reference"; and Kuyper, "all-embracing life system." Lowrie, *Those Who Teach in Christian Schools*, and many others, use "lens."

42. Sire, *Naming the Elephant*, 122. Sire's work was instrumental in popularizing the concept and identifying its practical benefit to the field of education.

43. Naugle, *Worldview*, 330. Naugle's work is extraordinary in its scope and detail regarding the history of the concept of worldview. He writes as a Christian philosopher and scholar, and he sees extraordinary practical value and power in this idea for the Christian church today. His work is often quoted by subsequent authors on the topic.

44. Sire, *Naming the Elephant*, 20.

45. Sire, *Universe Next Door*.

46. Naugle provides a partial list of the worldview-shaping influences, cited in Sire, *Naming the Elephant*, 46.

47. Naugle, cited in Sire, *Naming the Elephant*, 46.

48. Walsh and Middleton, *Transforming Vision*, 31–32.

49. Gaebelein, *Pattern of God's Truth*, 110–11.

50. Thiessen, *Teaching for Commitment*, 222.

51. Sire, cited in Walsh and Middleton, *Transforming Vision*, 169.

52. I owe further debt to Stephen Vryhof, *Between Memory and Vision*, for his work

on the role of a functional Christian community in helping pass down a family's most deeply held convictions to their children.

53. Moes and McCarthy, *Independent Schools*, 1989.

54. Cardus Education Survey (2011), 30.

55. Holmes, *Idea of a Christian College*, 59.

56. I am indebted to Naugle and Walsh and Middleton for their descriptions of the way the content of the Bible relates to the shape of a Christian worldview.

57. The surveys were strictly anonymous so I have no way to attribute the response to the individual who wrote it or my gratitude for doing so.

CHAPTER 5

58. Quoted in Riesen, *Piety and Philosophy*, 46.

59. Lewis *Mere Christianity*, 75.

60. Schindler, "School Atmosphere," 420.

61. Riesen, *Piety and Philosophy*, 73. Lockerbie writes, "To begin—and sadly so!—your school might stand out in many people's estimate if only because it takes more seriously than most Christian schools its mission—rather, its obligation—to be utterly and entirely committed to being *a school*," *Christian Paideia*, 7. This gives an idea just how deep this suspicion of academics goes and how much it undermines the mission of Christian schooling.

CHAPTER 6

62. Riesen, *Piety and Philosophy*, 95.

63. Naugle, *Worldview*, 339.

64. Noll, *Jesus Christ and the Life*, 2, 12.

65. Noll, *Jesus Christ and the Life*, 22.

66. On the influence of the various fields of knowledge upon the shape of worldview see Harris, *Integration of Faith and Learning*, especially chapters 3 and 4.

67. Naugle, *Worldview*, 289.

68. Quoted in Harris, *Integration of Faith and Learning*, 72.

CHAPTER 7

69. Augustine, *Confessions*, 3.

70. Buechner, *Wishful Thinking*, 104.

71. I first learned of this expression of the truth from Mark Brink, longtime senior Bible teacher at Evangelical Christian School in Memphis. Mark attributes it to a former friend and pastor named Dick Woodward, who used it in the context of what he referred to as four spiritual secrets. The words succinctly capture Paul's teaching in 2 Corinthians 12:8–10, leading to his declaration: "For when I am weak, then I am strong." The words attributed to St. Augustine capture the same truth: "Let your faith help you to realize . . . your utter insufficiency, and his all sufficiency."

72. Galatians 5:17. Here we are talking about very complex theological realities pertaining to the sinful nature and the new nature given at the new birth. The old nature is gone; what remains are the patterns of thinking, speaking, and acting that related to the old nature. The point of it all is to understand the entire process of spiritual formation from inception to maturity and to teach it to the students in our schools.

73. I have a particular passion to see the fruit of the Spirt define the goal or outcome of the work of spiritual formation rather than public displays of piety (e.g., prayers before a football game) or even morality (not drinking, smoking, dancing, etc.). The signs of a heart made new are the fruit of the Spirit expressed in relationship to others.

74. John Bunyan, *Pilgrim's Progress*, 23.

75. Matthew 7:24–27. The description of the house built upon the sand is at the end of Jesus's first major teaching session known as the "Sermon on the Mount." Jesus says, "Anyone who hears these words of mine and does NOT put them into practice, is like the man who built his house upon the sand."

76. The parable of the sheep and the goats in Matthew 25:31–46.

77. Riesen, *Piety and Philosophy*, 123. Thiessen, *Teaching for Commitment,* uses "the evangelistic nature of truth," 172.

CHAPTER 8

78. Vryhof, *Between Memory and Vision*, 4.

79. On this idea, Hekman cites the work of Sergiovanni, who writes that functional and effective school communities are "defined by their centers of values, sentiments, and beliefs that create a sense of 'we' from 'I.'" "Schools as Communities," 10.

80. Bryk et al. present an interesting study of the Christian-school community, capturing well the power of the distinctive school community contributing to student flourishing. *Catholic Schools and the Common Good*, 57, 247.

81. Hekman, "Schools as Communities," 7.

82. Similar to Sire's description of the term "plausibility structure" to identify the value of children receiving a clear and consistent induction into a shared system of values as the most common path toward rational autonomy, Hekman, and others (see Berger, in Thiessen, *Teaching for Commitment*, 250) identify the power of a community with shared values to facilitate growth toward rational autonomy.

83. Bryk et al., *Catholic Schools*, 57, 247.

84. Vryhof, *Between Memory and Vision*, 12.

85. Garber, *Fabric of Faithfulness*, 51–52.

86. Glenn, "School Distinctiveness and Why It Matters," 51.

87. Hoeksema, "Study of Dutch Calvinist School Distinctiveness," 129.

88. Gaebelein, *Pattern of God's Truth*, 37.

89. Hekman, "Schools as Communities," 14.

CHAPTER 9

90. Harris, *Integration of Faith and Learning*, 17–18.

91. Plantinga, *Engaging God's World*, 120.

92. Buechner, *Wishful Thinking,* 95.

93. Plantinga, *Engaging God's World,* 120. Cornelius Plantinga attributes the idea of shaping the occupation to the kingdom to the influential writings of Nicholas Wolterstorff.

94. Williamson, *Shorter Catechism* 1, 1.

Afterword

A Look to the Future of Christian Schooling

The twenty-first-century field of Christian schooling is the downstream expression of a very old idea. Actually, more than an idea, it flows from the deeply held belief, or conviction, that a comprehensive education for children must bring together the truth revealed in the study of the academic disciplines with the truth of the historic Christian faith, revealed in the words of Scripture and in the Word made flesh in the person of Jesus Christ. Owing to the cultivating work of generations of people who have gone before, this powerful idea has swelled into a worldwide movement.

Today this movement has taken root and is now increasing in strength fueled in large part by two essential factors. The first is a new and growing consensus of leaders eager to embrace a *clarified mission of Christian schooling*, casting off the hindrance of bad ideas and defining what it is we are trying to do in a way that is unified, compelling, distinctive, and that better prepares Christian schools to flourish in an increasingly competitive marketplace of private schools. The second is a *clarified vision for the global impact of Christian schooling* as our schools more effectively prepare students to be instruments of God's restoration by fulfilling their calling to any and every occupation and in so doing expand God's kingdom and glory to the ends of the earth, in increasing measure, and until Christ returns at the end of time. Come, Lord Jesus.

As we look to the future, there are two essential factors required for the twenty-first-century movement of Christian schooling to bear its full fruit around the globe. The first is for parents, caregivers, grandparents, and all charitable investors to identify the value of the life-shaping mission of Christian schooling and the power of its vision for global impact in a way that causes them to become strategic investors in Christian schools by giving their time, talents, and financial resources to create a legacy in the lives of children through (1) making it possible for students to attend and (2) enabling schools to flourish through challenging economic and social times. Our world needs Christian schools, and Christian people must cause the movement to thrive.

The final factor for Christian schools around the world to bear full fruit is for school leaders, practitioners, participants—all who believe in the idea of a Christian school—to come together and give their best in a unified, collaborative effort to translate the idea of a Christian school into practice so that our schools around the world become in truth the best expression of who we are and can be for the sake of Christ and our mission to our students. Translating the idea of Christian schooling to the practice of Christian schooling will also be the focus of volume 2 in this study.

Tom Stoner
Naperville, Illinois

Bibliography

Augustine. *On Christian Doctrine*. Indianapolis: Bobb-Merrill, 1958.

————. *Confessions*. Oxford: Oxford University Press, 1991.

The Belgic Confession of 1561, Article 2, translation approved, 2011, by the Christian Reformed Church. https://www.crcna.org/welcome/beliefs/confessions/belgic-confession.

Braley, James, Jack Layman, and Ray White, eds. *Foundations of Christian School Education*. Colorado Springs: Purposeful Design, 2003.

Bryk, Anthony, et al. *Catholic Schools and the Common Good*. Cambridge: Harvard University Press, 1993.

Buechner, Frederick. *Wishful Thinking: A Seeker's ABC*. San Francisco: HarperOne, 1993.

Bunyan, John. *The Pilgrim's Progress*. New York: Barnes & Noble Classics, 2005.

Cardus Education Survey (2011). https://cardus.ca/research/education/reports/cardus-education-survey-phas-i-report-2011/.

Chadwick, Ron. P. *Teaching and Learning: An Integrated Approach to Christian Education*. Old Tappan, NJ: Fleming H. Revell, 1982.

Eckel, M. *The Whole Truth: Classroom Strategies for Biblical Integration*. N.p.: Xulon, 2003.

Gaebelein, Frank. *The Pattern of God's Truth*. Whittier, CA: ACSI, 1954.

————. "Toward a Philosophy of Christian Education." In *An Introduction to Evangelical Christian Education*, edited by J. E. Hakes, 37–50. Chicago: Moody, 1968.

Garber, Stephen. *The Fabric of Faithfulness*. Downers Grove, IL: InterVarsity, 2007.

Glenn, Charles. L. "School Distinctiveness and Why It Matters." In *Building a Better School*, edited by Timothy P. Wiens and Kathryn L. Wiens, 49–79. Stonybrook, NY: Paideia, 2012.

————. "What Real Education Requires." *Journal of Education* 180.3 (1998) 41–50.

Graham, Donovan L. *Teaching Redemptively: Bringing Grace and Truth into Your Classroom*. Colorado Springs: Purposeful Design, 2003.

Harris, Robert A. *The Integration of Faith and Learning: a Worldview Approach*. Eugene, OR: Cascade, 2004.

Hekman, Bruce. "Schools as Communities of Grace: Flourishing as Living Water and Living Stones." In *Schools as Communities: Educational Leadership, Relationships, and the Eternal Value of Christian Schooling*, edited by James L. Drexler, 3–22. Colorado Springs: Purposeful Design, 2007.

Hirsch, E. D., Jr. *Validity in Interpretation*. New Haven: Yale University Press, 1967.

Hoeksema, Timothy. "A Study of Dutch Calvinist School Distinctiveness." PhD diss., UCLA, 1991.

Holmes, Arthur F. *All Truth Is God's Truth*. Grand Rapids: Eerdmans, 1977.

———. *The Idea of a Christian College*. Grand Rapids: Eerdmans, 1987.

Kienel, Paul. A. "The Philosophy of Christian School Education." In *Philosophy of Christian School Education*, edited by Paul Kienel et al., i–xvii. Colorado Springs: ACSI, 1995.

Lewis, C. S. "Is Theology Poetry?" Quebec City: Samizdat, 2014. http//www.samizdat.qc.ca/arts/lit/Theology=Poetry_CSL.pdf.17.

———. *Mere Christianity*. New York: Macmillan, 1960.

Lockerbie, D. Bruce. *A Christian Paideia: The Habitual Vision of Greatness*. Colorado Springs: Purposeful Design, 2005.

Lowrie, Roy W. *To Those Who Teach in Christian Schools*. Whittier, CA: ASCI, 1978.

Moes, Paul, and Mark McCarthy. "Independent Schools: What Works?" Unpublished monograph, Dordt College, 1989.

National Center for Education Statistics (NCES). http://nces.ed.gov/fastfacts/display.asp?id=55.

Naugle, David K. *Worldview: The History of a Concept*. Grand Rapids: Eerdmans, 2002.

Newman, John Henry. *The Idea of a University*. Dublin: UCD International Centre for Newman Studies, 2009.

Noll, Mark. *Jesus Christ and the Life of the Mind*. Grand Rapids: Eerdmans, 2011.

Parsons, P. F. *Inside America's Christian Schools*. Macon, GA: Mercer University Press, 1987.

Plantinga, Cornelius A. *Engaging God's World: A Christian Vision of Faith, Learning, and Living*. Grand Rapids: Eerdmans, 2002.

Riesen, Richard. A. *Piety and Philosophy: A Primer for Christian Schools*. Phoenix: ACW, 2002.

Schindler, C. E. "School Atmosphere and Relationships." In *Philosophy of Christian School Education*, edited by Paul Kienel et al., 413-27. Colorado Springs: ACSI, 1995.

Scholars Concerned About Advanced Placement History. From "Letter Opposing the 2014 APUSH Frameworks," June 2, 2015. https://www.nas.org/storage/app/media/images/documents/Historians_Statement.pdf.

Sire, James W. *Naming the Elephant: Worldview as a Concept*. Downers Grove, IL: IVP Academic, 2004.

———. *The Universe Next Door: A Basic Worldview Catalog*. Downers Grove, IL: InterVarsity, 2009.

Smith, Christian. *The Bible Made Impossible*. Grand Rapids: Brazos, 2011.

Spears, Paul D., and Steven R. Loomis. *Education for Human Flourishing: A Christian Perspective*. Downers Grove, IL: IVP Academic, 2008.

Thiessen, E. J. *Teaching for Commitment: Liberal Education, Indoctrination, and Christian Nurture*. Montreal & Kingston: Gracewing, 1993.

Vryhof, Steven C. *Between Memory and Vision: The Case for Faith-Based Schooling*. Grand Rapids: Eerdmans, 2004.

Walsh, Brian, and J. Richard Middleton. *The Transforming Vision: Shaping a Christian Worldview*. Downers Grove, IL: InterVarsity, 1984.

Williamson, G. I. *The Shorter Catechism* Volume 1. Phillipsburg, VA: P&R, 1970.

Wolterstorff, Nicholas P. *Educating for Life: Reflections on Christian Teaching and Learning*. Edited by G. G. Stronks and C. W. Joldersma. Grand Rapids: Baker Academic, 2002.

Subject and Author Index

Scripture Index